THESE
THREE

A BELIEVER'S GUIDE TO
FAITH, HOPE, & LOVE

Stay The course!

Wyatt House books may be ordered through booksellers or by contacting:

Wyatt House Publishing
399 Lakeview Dr. W.
Mobile, Alabama   36609

Because of the dynamic nature of the Internet, any web address or links contained in this book may have changed since publication and may no longer be valid.

Scripture quotations are from the English Standard Version unless otherwise noted.

Cover design by: Molly Peacock
Interior design by: Mark Wyatt

ISBN 13: 978-1-7326049-9-5

Printed in the United States of America

THESE THREE

A BELIEVER'S GUIDE TO FAITH, HOPE, & LOVE

ALAN FLOYD

Wyatt House Publishing
Mobile, Alabama

What people are saying about

THESE THREE

"My good friend and fellow pastor, Dr. Alan Floyd, has shared with us his newest book, "THESE THREE: Faith, Hope and Love!" We hear much in life about each of those words, and yet Alan Floyd instructs us, not only on their individual power, but how the three words are related and why they are mentioned so often in scripture. In my first reading, I was captured by the author's creative approach, coupled with the practical teaching that will encourage every reader. Alan provides us with his personal experiences with Faith, Hope and Love. He then adds the biblical truth and application to these three of the world's most powerful words... FAITH, HOPE and LOVE. My friend has given us a "Must Read" in "THESE THREE!" Well done!"

Larry Thompson
Pastor Emeritus of First Baptist Church,
Ft. Lauderdale, FL
Executive Director of Faith Foundry

"For many decades now, Cottage Hill Baptist Church has been a leading congregation in the Gulf Coast region. As it is also my home church, I have been delighted to see Dr. Alan Floyd leading this congregation forward with renewed mission and ministry vibrancy. This new book by Dr. Floyd, THESE THREE is a helpful unpacking of 1 Corinthians 13:13 wherein Paul says, 'So now faith, hope, and love abide, these three; but the greatest of these is love.' This work is bound to strengthen the spiritual life of most any believer, and serve as a beneficial small-group or congregational study."

Jason Allen
President, Midwestern Baptist Theological Seminary

"Over the course of my life as a Christian and college football coach I have read many faith-based and secular books on leadership. The words: Faith, Hope, and Love have come up in both of these environments. It was not until I read Alan Floyd's book, THESE THREE, did I realize the depth of Faith, Hope, and Love. His book has helped me to develop an increased maturity in my Christian life. I highly recommend this book to any Christian wanting to develop a deeper understanding of God's character and to anyone that is in a leadership role that wants to increase their effectiveness."

Tommy Bowden
Football Analyst
Former Head Football Coach, Clemson University

"Imagine a friend dropping by to show you a beautiful new, finely-tuned sports car. He raises the hood to show you the high horsepower engine as it idles smoothly. Then your friend mashes the gas to give you a sense of the vehicle's sheer power and force. Finally, your friend tosses you the keys and says, 'All this and more belongs to you.'

That's what my friend and yours, Alan Floyd, has done in his book THESE THREE. He lifts the hood and gives us all a glimpse of the engine that drives the victorious Christian life—faith, hope, and love. THESE THREE introduces us to Faith, Hope and Love simplified. Then Alan gives us a glimpse of what happens with the Holy Spirit 'mashes the gas' in our lives to reveal 'these three' amplified.

Then he 'tosses you the keys' to your own 30-day journey as you personalize faith, hope, and love in light of God's truth. This book is filled with practical insights and powerful truths. THESE THREE demystifies victorious living and shows how every believer in Christ is an overcomer by birthright. All the while Alan walks with you as a trusted friend and guide. This book is a delight to read and a gift that keeps on giving."

Andy Wood
Executive Leadership Coach
The LifeVesting Group

"Pastor Alan Floyd does a masterful job connecting the dots of Faith, Hope and Love. For new Christians, the examples and explanations will propel you forward in understanding one of the most well know verses in the Bible and how it profoundly impacts your life. For mature Christians, as you read you will visualize the connectivity in ways you possibly have overlooked in the past."

Sandy Stimpson
Mayor, City of Mobile, AL

"Often times in our Christian walk we hear so much about what we 'should do' and find ourselves discouraged and not knowing 'how to' walk things out in our daily lives. In THESE THREE, Pastor Alan rekindles that vision God so desires for us. He relates to the struggles we face personally in walking out God's plan. However, most encouragingly, he provides clear instruction on 'how to' be victorious in our walk of Faith, Hope and Love."

Marty Carrell
CEO, Women's Resource Center
Mobile, AL

"When we live out our Faith it always has a trickle down effect on those around us. THESE THREE is Alan Floyd's heart and has had a game-changing impact on the church he pastors in Mobile, Alabama. Cottage Hill has experienced the most amazing revitalization and under Alan's leadership, the church has become the gold standard for revitalization. THESE THREE is a major part of the foundation that has been laid for this incredible story. This book should be a part of any pastor's library that is wanting to see a resurgence. Do yourself a favor buy it! Read it!"

Kelly Green
President, Kelly Green Global

"Faith, Hope, and Love. With clarity, Dr. Floyd takes the reader on a deep journey to understand the connectivity of these terms in the life of a follower of Jesus. THESE THREE reflects a life given to discover the depths of Jesus Christ. This is not only about entering His kingdom, but maturing in His kingdom so that we all might be more like Jesus, laying hold of the treasures of scripture which reveal who He is and what we can be as subjects in His Kingdom."

Bill Hightower
Senator, State of Alabama

"THESE THREE...I LOVE it! Dr. Floyd has a real gift of taking powerful, sometimes hard to understand, Biblical truths and making them understandable and applicable. This book mirrors his preaching style; organized impactful content sprinkled with humor and personal stories. That's is a great recipe for hungry listeners!"

Dennis Hayford
Area Director, South Alabama
Fellowship of Christian Athletes

"As someone who has spent years in full-time ministry,

I've noticed that Pastor Alan is the first one to encourage, support and love on people. Now, being a businessman and entrepreneur, I love my interactions with him even more - he has a gift and anointing to turn things around. He can take a seemingly hopeless situation and breathe life into it, It's been truly remarkable to watch. He's without a doubt a 'turn-around guy.' Take time to read this very important word applicable to us all. He explains deep truths that when understood and walked in will yield a fruit that is unmistakably a follower of Jesus Christ. As believers, this is how we are called to live. Let's be full of faith, live with hope, and never let our love die."

Jeff Roberts
President and Founder, Yellowhammer Coffee

"We've all heard the phrase 'everyone knows, but do they *know*?' This is certainly an example of the famous Bible passage the Apostle Paul penned in 1 Corinthians 13. Everyone knows the love chapter, right? And the famous benediction, 'So now faith, hope, and love abide, these three; but the greatest of these is love.' How exciting for all to know and grasp this gospel bombshell! Pastor Alan Floyd unpacks the glorious truth of what faith, hope and love look like when a Christ follower is living out these gospel virtues. The way Pastor Alan leads the reader to dial in to each one, wow! Truth is, everyone needs to know about, THESE THREE It's inspiring when you imagine what it will be like when a movement begins- Christ followers living out faith, hope and love. When this happens, without a doubt, all will know! Be blessed by Dr. Floyd's new book."

Jeff Crook
Lead Pastor, Christ Place Church
Flowery Branch, GA

"THESE THREE a powerful, biblical book of these great

truths of faith, hope, and love are explained and applied to our life in a marvelous way. Dr. Alan Floyd with great insight makes these wonderful truths come alive and show how they are a part of the daily life of a follower of Jesus. As I read it, I was blessed, encouraged, and my faith was strengthened. You will be blessed by this book!"

Fred H. Wolfe
Founding Pastor, Luke 4:18 Fellowship
Mobile, AL

To Kathy,

My wife and best friend.

"Happy is the man who finds a true friend, and far happier is he who finds that true friend in his wife."
                                        -Franz Schubert

CONTENTS

INTRODUCTION

How do I live out my faith? What does it really look like, not on paper, but lived out in flesh and blood? That's not a new question, of course. Even the early church, the first church struggled with what it meant to live out their belief in Christ Jesus. In 1 Corinthians 13:13, Paul links together the three basic ideas of our Christian beliefs: faith, hope, and love: "So now faith, hope, and love abide, these three; but the greatest of these is love." The writer of Hebrews does the same thing in Hebrews 6:10-12, "For God is not unjust so as to overlook your work and the love that you have shown for his name in serving the saints, as you still do. And we desire each one of you to show the same earnestness to have the full assurance of hope until the end, so that you may not be sluggish, but imitators of those who through faith and patience inherit the promises." Again in Colossians 1:4-5a, "since we heard of your faith in Christ Jesus and of the love that you have for all the saints, because of the hope laid up for you in heaven."

Two other passages, found in Paul's first letter to the Thessalonians, and the Apostle Peter's first letter, contain this magnificent trinity. In other words, the link between faith, hope, and love served as a summary of the Christian life. This is how the first Christians understood what Jesus intended for their lives. In the same way that we say, "I believe in the Father, the Son, and the Holy Spirit," we outline the Christian life by affirming the essential connection between faith, hope, and love in the life of every Christian.

Over 25 years of serving as a pastor, I have seen the inextricable bond between faith, hope, and love in practice through every stage of the Christian walk. I have also heard the same question in many forms from new believers, returning seekers, and seasoned saints alike: "So what does God desire of me? How do we live it out?"

God's desire, God's very best plan for you, is that over time you will become a person of deeper faith, greater love, and unwavering eternal hope. This book is not intended to be an exhaustive study, but seeks to answer those questions using these three: faith, hope, and love, as our guide. My prayer is that when our time together is done, you will be well on your way to being the person God created you to be.

FAITH goes up the stairs
that **LOVE** has built
and looks out the windows
which **HOPE** has opened.

- *Charles H. Spurgeon*

SECTION 1

SIMPLIFY

Chapter One

FAITH

"I believe the promises of God enough
to venture an eternity on them."

- Isaac Watts

What does God desire of us? How do we live it out? In 1 Corinthians 13:13, we see God's simplified plan for us, "So now faith, hope, and love abide, these three; but the greatest of these is love." If we were to narrow it down, what does God want *from* us and *for* us? Very simple: Faith, Hope and Love. What does faith look like simplified? What does faith look like when it is lived out, amplified in and through your life?

For centuries, followers of Jesus have been given many different names. Saints, believers, followers of the way, Christians, disciples—all are names Christ-followers have been called over the centuries. Each of these names gives a distinctive quality of the Christian believers' life. In 1 John

5:4-5, John suggests another name for Christians: *Overcomers*. He writes, "For everyone who has been born of God overcomes the world. And this is the victory that has overcome the world—our faith. Who is it that overcomes the world except the one who believes that Jesus is the Son of God?"

In three different occasions—in just these verses—we are called *overcomers*. And this isn't the only place where Christians are described this way. For example, in Romans 8:37 Paul said, "No, in all these things we are more than conquerors through him who loved us." To the Christians in Corinth in 1 Corinthians 15:57, Paul wrote, "But thanks be to God, who gives us the victory through our Lord Jesus Christ."

A Christian is *one who overcomes*. It's clear that God's desire for the Christian is that we would overcome.

THE PROBLEM

Now honestly, do you feel much like an overcomer? I believe most Christians don't. In my daily life as a pastor, in my interactions with others, I find that many Christians are discouraged and feel that something is standing in the way of living the Christian life to the fullest. Well, that something is the world. In the context of 1 John 5:4-5, when John calls the Christian an overcomer, he says that the believer overcomes "the world." Our problem is the world. Three times in these two verses we are told what the problem is, what it is that is keeping us from overcoming. It's the world. But what does that mean?

What is the world? The world is Satan and his plans. The world is sin and its pressure. The world is suffering

22

and its pain. The world is sensuality and its pleasure. The world is anything and everything that stands in opposition to God. What does the world do? It attempts to destroy our Christian witness. It attempts to distort our desires. It attempts to dilute our interest in God's Word. It attempts to squeeze us into its mold (see Rom. 12:2). Simply stated, the world seeks to keep you away from God and His plan for you.

THE PROMISE

The good news is that while verses 4 and 5 clearly tell us the problem, they also give us a promise—we WILL overcome. Although the world is in the way, God's promise is for you to overcome. That means we do not have to be defeated by the devil. We do not have to be disgraced by sin. We do not have to be destroyed by suffering. We do not have to be distracted by sensuality. We can win the victory! We can overcome! It is a written guarantee of God!

But is God trustworthy? Surely, you've had people who didn't keep their promises. In fact, not long ago a man made a promise to me that he would do something, but he didn't keep his promise. I knew when he promised it that chances were slim that he would actually fulfill his promise. You see, you cannot really trust a promise unless you know who made that promise. Right? You must go beyond the promise to the one who made the promise. Here's what you should know: God always stands behind His word! Psalm 9:10 says, "Those who know your name will trust in you, for you, Lord, have never forsaken those who seek you." God has NEVER made a promise He didn't keep. You can rest in the knowledge that if God says you can overcome, you can do it.

THE PRINCIPLE

This promise of victory, however, belongs to those who apply the principle. What is the principle that will enable us to realize the guarantee and be overcomers? John answers that in 1 John 5:4. He says, "This is the victory that has overcome the world, our faith." We overcome by FAITH. Through faith, we experience the victorious Christian life. But what is faith?

Faith Described

Some years ago, when I was pastoring in Atlanta, Georgia, I went to "the busiest airport in the world" to fly to a speaking engagement. As I drove to the airport I noticed the darkening and swirling of the clouds and the announcer on the radio spoke of the threat of tornadoes in the area. To tell the truth, I wasn't looking forward to flying through that weather. As I boarded the plane, I saw a man I recognized, David Johnston. He was a pilot who was a member of our church and dear friend. When I spotted him, I know my face lit up. I said, "Man, this is great! Brother, I'm so glad to see you on this plane and know you're going to be flying this baby, getting me there safe!" He looked at me and said the strangest thing: "Man, I was just thinking that I'm not looking forward to flying this thing tonight, and I really felt better when I saw you get on board!" Well, we were a couple of fellows who didn't have the right kind of faith that night. Our faith was in each other, and it wasn't too steady!

All of life is lived on faith and every person has faith in something. We open a can of soup and eat it because we have faith that it is not harmful to us. We get on a plane and sit back with confidence because we have faith that the pilot who is flying the plane knows what he is doing. Think about it, we go to a doctor whose name we cannot pronounce; they give us a prescription we cannot read; we take it to a pharmacist we do not know; they give us medicine that we do not understand... and yet we take it, all on faith! To have faith means *to trust*.

It reminds me of the story of a man who came to a baseball game a little late. When he got there and asked one of the boys in the dugout what the score was, the boy replied, "Seventeen to nothing!" "Wow," the man replied, "I bet you're discouraged." "Why should we be discouraged?" asked the little leaguer. "We haven't even gotten up to bat yet!" That is the spirit of one who lives by faith.

So what is Christian faith? What does that look like? Even though there is no precise definition of faith in the Bible, the book of Hebrews contains a mighty description of faith, making clear what faith is in the life of the believer. Hebrews 11:1 says, "Faith is being sure of what we hope for and certain of what we do not see." "Being sure" is like putting supports on. That is the word used here. Faith is having a prop under you, something to support you. Faith is standing under what we hope for, and being certain; having proof or conviction; it is the outward display of an inner commitment.

That's what Noah had when God told him to build a ship, an ark, and to gather two of every kind of animal before the rains started to flood the earth. Many people don't realize that Noah had never seen rain, because it had never happened before. He didn't really know what "rain" meant. On the dry land he built that ark, then he loaded all the animals on it and it still hadn't rained. What happened? God spoke. He stood under what God said, with proof and conviction—not that it had rained, but that God had said it. And so he outwardly displayed what his heart believed. Faith is being sure of what we hope for, and certain of what we do not see.

The Origin of Faith

What is the origin of faith? The Bible tells us in Romans 10:16 where it comes from. "Not all the Israelites accepted the good news. For Isaiah says, *'Lord, who has believed our message?'* Consequently, faith comes from hearing the message..."

Faith comes from God. Any faith that I have, or that you have, is God-given. We don't just suddenly say, "I'm going to have faith." God must give it.

So how does one have enough faith to become a Christian? How can I put my trust in a Man whom I've never seen, who lived in a country across the ocean, two thousand years ago, and who tells me in a Book that He is the Son of God? How can I have the faith to believe that, and to believe that when I die, He is going to take my soul to heaven, to live with Him forever? That faith has to come from God. The devil can't give you that kind of faith. You can't work it up, or you would have already believed. Your belief in God, your salvation experience, and then your desire to obey Him, in the Christian walk—is all from God.

The origin of faith is God; the instrument is the Bible. "Faith comes from hearing the message, and the message is heard through the word of God." God resurrects this faith in our hearts and minds. We place our faith in what God has said in the Bible. It is not something we work up, but something God hands down.

It's like when my two sons were young and they wanted to give their mom something for Christmas or her birthday. They'd come to me for the money or to take them shopping. Then they wrote on the card, "To Mommy, with love," and signed their names. Now, they didn't have the money to buy that gift, although they spent it and gave the gift as if it were theirs. It was Daddy who made it all possible. Living by faith is exactly the same. It's all from God. We didn't have it or get it--He gives it to us and we give it back in obedience, although we had nothing to do with getting it originally. It comes from God and from knowing the Scripture.

The Object of Faith

If the origin of faith is God, what is the object of faith? Hebrews 12:2 tells us clearly that the object is Jesus Christ. The writer of Hebrews says, "We look to Jesus, the Author and Finisher of our faith." Here's a truth you can hold onto: your faith is no better than the object of your faith. If I say that I believe the chair I'm sitting in can hold me up, I have faith in the chair. I believe it will hold me if I sit in it. But suppose that when I sat in the chair it collapsed. It wouldn't matter how much faith I had in the chair, I would still be sitting on the floor!

Faith in any other object will not save us, no matter how much faith we have. Faith in your own faith is not enough; faith in what some philosopher said is not enough. Faith in any religion is not enough. There is only one worthy object of faith, and that is Jesus Christ. We look to Jesus, the Author and Finisher of our faith.

your faith is no better than the object of your faith

I am blessed to be married to a very beautiful woman. Like most of us, I have married 'way above' myself! Early in my marriage, I would have the occasional friend ask me, "Do you worry about Kathy cheating on you?" I would always respond, "No, not a bit." Shaking their head, they would say, "Well, you are a man of faith." I would respond, "No, I have a wonderful wife." You see, they were not complimenting me, but complimenting her. Let me say it again, your faith is no better than the object of your faith. To have a great faith, is to have a great God!

The Outcome of Faith

Our God longs to show Himself mighty on behalf of people who trust Him. Remember, faith is the "lever" by which our needs are met, whatever they may be. Let me remind you of what Jesus said: "Therefore I tell you, whatever you ask for in prayer, believe that you have received it, and it will be yours." *(Mark 11:24)* "According to your faith will it be done to you." *(Matt. 9:29)*

Faith goes beyond reason. That doesn't mean it ignores reason, but faith goes a step beyond reason. Reason can be treason! So many people can't accept things they cannot see, touch, smell, hear, outsmart, or define literally. Faith takes that extra step. It's not a leap into the dark, but into the light, based on the faithfulness of God's revelation of Himself and His movement in my life.

Reasoning is important, but limited. For instance, when David went to fight Goliath, reason said, "Hey man, you can't win!" This teenage boy walked up to a man who was at least nine feet tall (some scholars believe he was eleven feet tall!), who had the entire nation of Israel trembling. This shepherd boy came out to fight him, they tried to put armor on him and he said, "I don't need that. Give me five smooth stones and my sling-shot and let me at him." Reason said he was crazy, but David had faith. By the way, if you're wondering why David grabbed five stones if he had the faith to kill Goliath, you need to realize that Goliath had four other brothers! So he said to Goliath, "I come to you in the name of the Lord God of Israel!" His faith was not in that sling-shot. He could have missed! His faith was not in the army behind him, because they were scared. This boy took on Goliath, because he said, "I come in the name of the Lord God of Israel." Faith moved beyond reason in order to enable him to win the battle.

So it is when we place our faith in God. We believe God can do something beyond reason. That is why many believers have difficulty in giving money to the work of the church. They try to reason it out: "I've got so much income, so much outflow; therefore I can't make it work." They are living by reason and not by faith. That's why God can't bless them.

How do you get out of financial trouble? Begin to believe God and obey Him, then you'll begin to give. As you discipline your life in stewardship, giving at least a tithe at first, and then going beyond later, you will see that God will begin to shape up the rest of your money. You will find it lasting longer than you thought it could. You will check yourself before you go and buy something wrong. You will watch the amount of money you put on that credit card and you will find yourself making that money go farther, because you are believing God to be your source—not human reasoning.

The origin of faith is God, the object of faith is God, the outcome of faith is God. When we believe Him, we can go beyond reason. We also go beyond emotion. It takes more than emotion. That's why the Scripture says we "'walk not by sight (reason, or feeling), but by faith." *(2 Cor. 5:7)*

Have you ever watched a football team when it's first running onto the field, all fired up for the ball game, giving each other high-fives, slapping each other on the back? Then they get into the huddle and go out to the 50-yard line all fired up. They're the underdogs who are supposed to be beaten by four touchdowns. But when you watch their spirit, you say, "Man, they are tough! They're really hyped up! They're going to win this game! Look at their enthusiasm, they've got all the emotion in the world!" But after the first quarter, they are behind by 30 points, just getting the pants beat off of them! They are living by emotion. If emotion can win the game, they would have been on top, but they got whipped because emotion cannot take the place of faith in life—or in the football game.

Just like in football, we don't win by our feelings in life. Sometimes when I get up to preach, I don't really feel like it. Sometimes I'm really fired up, but other times I'm not. Sometimes I say, "Lord, I am going to praise You, not by feeling, but by faith!" When we live and minister by faith instead of feeling, not being run by our emotions, we begin to have a more objective, balanced life and ministry.

In life, truth is not what our emotions say, truth is what God says. Our object of faith is God, so faith is interpreted as being from God and supported by God . It is proof of and the assurance of, standing under the fact that God gives faith. God is the object of faith in Jesus Christ and the outcome of faith is built not on what I think or what my reason says, but on what God says.

What is your obstacle, your impossible situation? Faith enables us to overcome in one of two ways: sometimes, by the mighty power of God, faith simply obliterates the impossibility. Faith moves the mountain out of the way. Sometimes, there are circumstances so bottom-line, so non-negotiable, so changeless, that the impossibility will never move. Faith changes me, so that in the face of the impossible, I am not under it, but over it. I am not a victim *of* it, but a victor *over* it. Faith moves me over the mountain!

Faith Delivered

What exactly does faith do? It delivers a promise. The promise delivered to the saints of old, through faith, is available to us! "Therefore, the promise comes by faith, so that it may be by grace and may be guaranteed to all Abraham's offspring—not only to those who are of the law but also to those who are of the faith of Abraham. He is the father of us all." *(Romans 4:16) NIV*

Paul is saying that if we believe as Abraham believed, we receive as Abraham received. This is of great encouragement because Abraham was not perfect. He had his faults. The emphasis here, though, is not on his faults, but his faith. So Paul says that if you believe, you will have faith like Abraham. You will receive what he received. What did he receive?

The Present of God

"The promise comes by faith, so that it may be by grace..." In other words, without faith, you will never know God's grace. Grace is defined as "the unmerited love and favor of God." It is a gift, a present given to us by God through faith. God's Grace is available to you, by faith. Please make this clear in your mind: unbelief holds grace prisoner. In other words, faith opens the door to God's amazing grace.

The Presence of God

When David Livingstone, the great missionary to Africa, was called back to London to receive an honor, he was presented the award before a vast gathering of well-wishers. Someone asked him how he had been able to endure it when the natives rose up against him and when the powers of darkness seemed ready to overwhelm him. He opened his well-worn Bible and said, "Let me share with you the verse that helped me make it through: 'Lo, I am with you always, even to the end of age'" *(Matt. 28:20)*.

The promise of His presence provides victory! Because of our faith, we know that God is with us every step of the way.

The Power of God

Faith delivers to us the power of God. Many years ago, when I was a seminary student serving a church in Texas, I visited a rancher who had recently joined our church. As I approached his home, I saw a man dressed in black pumping water with a hand pump. The water was pouring out into a watering trough. I thought to myself, "That man is really pumping that water!" When I got closer, I discovered that it wasn't a real man after all, but man-shaped plywood connected to the pump. The pump was actually powered by electricity. I laughed as I realized that the man was not pumping the water, the water was pumping the man!

unbelief holds grace prisoner

It is the same with us. From a distance, some may look at us and say, "That guy has power. Look at how he lives. He is really living for God!" But when they get closer, they realize that it is actually God who is living in us.

The power of God is ample and available. Through faith, we plug into that power, and it begins to move through us. The power provides victory, because "the one who is in you is greater than the one who is in the world" *(I John 4:4)*.

The Plan of God

What is the plan of God? Victory. His plan is for you to be an overcomer, to overcome the world. God has initiated a plan in this world that is permanent and eternal.

The things of this world will someday fade away, and every knee will bow before Jesus Christ. Faith reminds us that the final victory belongs to God, and therefore faith encourages us to keep going.

Do you want to live life every day knowing that God is with you? Guiding you? Holding your hand? Do you want to know that God will meet your needs? That you will, in Christ, win the victory? Do you have faith? If you have faith, if you live out faith, you will experience what God desires. You will be an *overcomer*.

Chapter Two

HOPE

"Without Christ there is no hope."
- Charles Spurgeon

We live life in three dimensions. You have a past, present and a future. The Christian experience has three dimensions as well. FAITH, HOPE and LOVE. These are the characteristics, the basics of the Christian life. The word, FAITH, is the word that deals with our past. We come to Christ as sinners. We come to Christ in our sin. But by faith we receive what the Lord Jesus Christ did for us when He died for us on Calvary's cross. By faith, we reach back to the finished work of Jesus Christ and His shed blood for us on the cross. That's faith. The word, LOVE, describes the present dimension of our faith. Our present existence as believers and our present lifestyle as believers should be characterized by love.

But the word that describes the future dimension of our faith (Christian experience) is this word HOPE. Our Christian faith looks to the future and the word that describes that for us is the word, hope. Hope refers to the future dimension of the Christian life. We see how these three work together in Col. 1:3-5, "We always thank God, the Father of our Lord Jesus Christ, when we pray for you, since we heard of your faith in Christ Jesus and of the love that you have for all the saints, because of the hope laid up for you in heaven."

The Christian life that is produced by the Gospel is completed by three ingredients: FAITH, HOPE, and LOVE. In other words, we are to Rely on Faith, Remain in Love, and Rest in Hope!

Think of hope as "the confident expectation of something good." In the Old Testament, words like "refuge" and "shelter" take the place of "hope"—meaning hope is the thing that protects us when everything else around us crumbles). So, because hope is about this future dimension in the Christian life, we ask, "Lord, what does my future hold as a believer?" In the Bible there are three beautiful pictures to help us understand HOPE.

we are to Rely on Faith, Remain in Love, and Rest in Hope!

HOPE IS THE ANCHOR OF OUR SOUL

"We have this as a sure and steadfast anchor of the soul, a

hope that enters into the inner place behind the curtain."
(Hebrews 6:19)

Hope is unseen. It's as hard to pin down as faith. It's intangible, hidden from our eyes. So it seems strange to associate something so elusive with an anchor. Anchors are big, hooked, and heavy. We associate anchors with sailors, ships, and seagulls. The writer of Hebrews isn't saying that hope is a literal anchor. He's drawing a comparison between what an anchor does for its ship and what hope does for our souls.

The purpose of an anchor was vital to the welfare of ships. It was the anchor that provided stability. It was the anchor that kept the ship from drifting, when the storms blew, the winds howled, and the waves tossed. If the ship was anchored, it was safe and secure. So the anchor became a symbol of hope. It became a symbol of security. The Bible says we have a "sure anchor". Our anchor is the Lord Jesus Christ.

It is a Sure Anchor

The word, *sure* in the verse means it is a *firm* anchor. It is a solid anchor. Anchors have to be firm and solid. If they don't hold on, then there is no security there. An anchor in the sea would go down, down, down, to the depths of the sea and would finally find its resting place in the dark murky waters on the bottom of the sea. Our soul's anchor does not go downward, our soul's anchor goes up, up, beyond the starry skies. Up into the very throne of God, into the unseen holy of holies itself. Our anchor is secured in heaven. We are secure because our anchor is already in heaven. It is a sure anchor.

It is a Steadfast Anchor

The word, steadfast, in Hebrews 6:19 indicates it is "fixed." It can hold up under the pressure. People are under a lot of pressure today. People are cracking under the pressure all of the time; but if you have your life anchored in the Lord Jesus Christ you can weather the storms. I don't know what winds are blowing against you, but you have Jesus Christ, He's your anchor, you are going to make it through. You are coming out on the other side. Let the winds blow! Let the storms rage!

For example, James 1:6 tells us that doubt can toss us like a cork bobbling wildly in the ocean's waves. Ephesians 4:14 says that newbies in the faith can be tossed and carried by the wind of false teaching. Hope stabilizes our emotions, putting us on an even keel. Our souls know the full range of feeling – happiness, worry, sorrow, curiosity, pity, sincerity, fear. God's people sometimes go through unimaginable things. They go through all kinds of heartaches, pressures, and tensions. Yet in the midst of tumultuous emotions, hope holds us steadfast.

if you have your life anchored in the Lord Jesus Christ, you can weather the storms

Our anchor is both sure and steadfast. The verse goes on to say, "enters into the inner place behind the curtain" *(Hebrews 6:19)*. Of course, we know that within the veil, or curtain, of the temple is where the holy of holies was. That veil was right in front of the holy of holies and the high priest would go within that veil. The Bible says that our anchor, the Lord Jesus Christ, has entered within the veil.

In Biblical days, ships would come to the harbor but sometimes they would come at low tide. There would be a sand bar at the opening of the harbor, and because it was low tide, the ship couldn't go in. So they would send a man in a boat to take the anchor, and in his little boat, he would go on into the harbor and drop that anchor of the ship on into the harbor. There sat the ship outside the harbor. The anchor was on the inside of the harbor. The winds might blow. The storms might come. The waves might beat against the ship. But the ship would stand because the anchor was already in the harbor. Then, when the time was right, when the high tide came in, and the water would rise, the ship would enter where the anchor was. The anchor was the guarantee that the ship would go in where the anchor was located.

One of these days, when the old tide of death sweeps across our bow, we'll go into glory and be with our anchor, the Lord Jesus Christ.

HOPE IS THE ARMOR OF OUR SALVATION

"But since we belong to the day, let us be sober, having put on the breastplate of *faith* and *love*, and for a helmet the *hope* of salvation." *(1 Thess. 5:8)*

There it is again... do you see it? Faith, Hope, Love. Remember, *armor* for Paul was more than pictures from daily life with the nearly omnipresent Roman Legionnaires.

Armor for him was a way that he put together the elements of what our life in Christ is to be all about. In Ephesians 6:13-17, Paul gives a more exhaustive list of the combat equipment in almost the order that it was originally issued to a Roman Legionnaire and also the order in which those soldiers would put it on.

Historians tell us that the Roman Legionnaire was invincible as long as he followed the code of conduct of the great Imperial Warfare Guide of the Roman Emperors. But after the time of Paul and the centuries that followed, there were increasing defeats. Historians also tell us from journals of the battles that the Roman Legionnaires were becoming indifferent to wearing the armor. That armor was hard to wear—it was bulky and heavy. Those helmets were hot and stuffy. Often men would go out unprepared, unfitted for the battle, and the invincible Roman legions began to be defeated.

In the church today, when we trusted Christ, we received Him as our armor. Paul told the Romans to "put on the Lord Jesus Christ" *(Rom. 13:14)*. By faith, put on the armor and trust God for the victory. Once and for all, we have put on the armor at the moment of salvation. But there must be a daily renewal, a daily fitting, a daily tightening down of that armor. Just as King David took off his armor and returned to his palace, he was in greater danger than when he was on the battlefield. We see this in 2 Samuel 11, when he fell prey to his lusts and committed adulterous sin with Bathsheba. Therefore, we are never out of reach of Satan's devices, so we must never be without the whole armor of God.

A Roman soldier would never go to battle without a helmet. That would be foolish. Helmets were made in two different ways: leather, with some patches of metal on it, or solid cast metal. An archaeologist who unearthed burial grounds of Roman soldiers found a broad 3-foot-long sword. This type of sword has a handle on it like a baseball bat. It was kind of swung around in battle. In fact, there are men in the battlefield graves whose skulls are cleaved right down in half because obviously they had not put on their helmet. These dull yet powerful, broad-bladed swords were swung around on the battlefield. They were very dangerous without a helmet. So the Christian soldier must have his helmet of assurance of salvation.

> ## *a lack of assurance in our life leaves open the door for defeat*

Nearly any object in the battlefield can immobilize us if we are not assured of all that God has done. Therefore, the warning of the helmet of salvation is that a lack of assurance in our life leaves open the door for defeat. A soldier was never far from his helmet. Nearly any object on the battlefield could immobilize a soldier if his head was unprotected. So to the Christian soldier the meaning of the helmet is assurance of salvation. *WARNING: Lack of assurance brings defeat!*

Vital to Our Present Safety

The battleground of Satan is our mind. The place where he

brings doubt and despair and defeat to us is in the mind. It is an invisible war. That battle is vicious and intense. It is unrelenting and unfair because Satan never plays fair. It is so intense because your greatest asset is your mind. Whatever gets your *mind* gets *you*. So one of the most important things we need to learn and teach others is how to guard, strengthen, and renew our minds—because the battle for sin always starts in the mind. That is where Satan can get the inroads. It is vital to "stand" as referenced in Eph. 6:14: "Stand therefore, having fastened on the belt of truth, and having put on the breastplate of righteousness."

The helmet and sword are the last two pieces a soldier takes up. A helmet, being hot and uncomfortable, would be put on by a soldier only when he faced impending danger. Sometimes the soldiers waited too long. Instead of putting on that hot and uncomfortable helmet at the first sound of battle, they would leave it strapped to their belt while they prepared everything else. Then, before they knew it, an arrow shot randomly in the air, or a projectile from a catapult would strike and kill them. Why? They didn't have their helmet on!

This is something you must do. This is something that I must do. None of the pieces of armor just fall out of heaven and clothe us. We must see take responsibility for it ourselves, making sure that we are properly armed for the battle. "Stand therefore" refers to standing against the devil's attacks. The helmet is vital because it is our present safety from the attacks of Satan.

Vital to Our Future Deliverance

The "helmet of salvation" is only mentioned three times in the Bible (Ephesians 6, 1 Thessalonians, and Isaiah 59). It is amazing how wonderfully God pulls those three together. Again, in 1 Thessalonians 5:8: "But since we belong to the day, let us be sober, having put on the breastplate of *faith* and *love*, and for a helmet the *hope* of salvation."

Our helmet has two elements. In Ephesians 6 it is a present protection from Satan's attacks. In 1 Thessalonians 5:8, "the hope of salvation as a helmet" refers to our future deliverance. Remember, our salvation is actually in three parts.

First, we were saved from the penalty of sin on the cross. The instant you and I by faith trusted Jesus Christ, the penalty of sin was defeated by His sacrifice for us. But the second realm of salvation lasts from our spiritual birth to the moment Christ comes for us in the clouds or calls us through death, and that is the deliverance from the power of sin. We bring great glory to God every time we say "NO" to sin. You want to glorify God? Just say "NO" to sin where you live. The instant we do that, we are defeating and overcoming the power of sin in our lives every day.

The third realm, the future aspect of salvation, means no presence of sin. Some day, when we are with Christ, there will be no more temptation. Satan will no longer attack us because he will be forever consigned to the Lake of Fire! The helmet of salvation in 1 Thessalonians 5:8 references the future hope of our salvation: our deliverance from the body of this sin. As the "day of the Lord" draws near, we should be personally alert, as well as properly armed in preparation of that day. So the helmet of salvation is vital, today and tomorrow!

HOPE IS THE ASSURANCE OF OUR STRENGTH

"Be of good courage, and He shall strengthen your heart, all you who hope in the Lord." *Psalm 31:24 (NKJV)*

Hope strengthens us. God promises that while we wait, our hope will serve as an assurance of divine strength. We know that our Lord will come back, we just don't know when. Waiting can be difficult. There's probably nothing more depressing than a waiting room! Doctor's offices and emergency rooms come immediately to mind. Or do you remember the last time you had to update your driver's license? Take a number. All we can do is settle down in our chair and prepare ourselves to endure the wait. It's hard to wait, isn't it?

> "but those who hope in the Lord will renew their strength. They will soar on wings like eagles; they will run and not grow weary, they will walk and not be faint." *Isaiah 40:31 (NIV)*

The NIV translates the Hebrew word *qavah* as HOPE. The KJV and ESV translate it as *wait*. The word "hope" and the word "wait" are exactly the same word in Hebrew. The definition of word "qavah" is "to wait, to hope, to expect." The meaning conveys anticipation. It is the same type of waiting or hoping that children do on Christmas morning in anticipation for their mom and dad to get out of bed so they can open their presents.

But what does it mean to wait on the Lord, or to hope in the Lord? He says it is because human strength will always fail. When we examine human strength, we see that it has many forms. First of all, there is physical strength. This strength can be very formidable, even impressive. There can also be psychological or mental strength. There are those who can develop, stretch, and educate their mind. Then there is emotional strength, the strength of the human will. People can develop their will to be very, very determined. But all forms of human strength have limitations. No matter how strong you may be physically, no matter how strong you may be mentally, no matter how strong you may be emotionally, all human strength has its limits. This is a fact that every person has to face at some time in their life.

> *The Christian Life is the exchanged life*

What do you do when physical, psychological, or emotional strength is gone? Well, human strength can be exchanged for divine strength. Isaiah 40:31 tells us "those who hope in the Lord will renew their strength." Another word for "renew" is exchange. The Christian life is the *exchanged* life. In the Christian life, I exchange my life for Jesus' life. It is giving my life to Jesus and Jesus giving His life to me. I get a lot better deal than Jesus gets. Amen? I give Him my life, but He gives me His life. He lives His life through me. Those who wait on the Lord will exchange their strength. This is God's answer.

What are the results of waiting on the Lord? Notice again in Isaiah 40:31 that he said "they will soar on wings like eagles."

Soaring Power

I believe the writer is saying if you wait on the Lord, eventually there will be soaring power..."They will soar on wings like eagles." I read recently that eagles fly normally around 50 miles an hour. But when they fly into a storm, the air lifts them higher and faster so that, in a storm, they fly twice as fast and twice as high. They fly up to 100 miles per hour in a storm! As we wait on the Lord, when the storm comes, God causes His people to have soaring power. He gives us a lift, causes us to soar in the face of the storm. He makes us soar high! He gives the strength to soar higher and faster. He provides soaring power for the storms of life... soaring on wings like eagles.

Strengthening Power

Then Scripture says there will be *strengthening power*..."they will run and not grow weary." The truth is, there are times in our life that are very stressful. There are times when we face extraordinary challenges and opportunities. Sometimes it is when our children are small, or when our job demands more of us. We are so busy; there are so many things to do. It seems like we don't have the time to do it all. God says if we wait upon Him, He'll give us strength to run and get the job done. In the most stressful time of life, God says we'll have that strength to run and not grow weary.

The Bible says of Philip, in Acts chapter 8, that he was in a busy time of life when the spirit of God was using him in a tremendous way. Philip was in Samaria preaching the gospel. Suddenly the Lord spoke to Philip and said, "I want you to leave Samaria and go down to the desert. I've got a job for you to do down there." God, in the spirit, took him down to the desert. There came a chariot through the desert and the spirit said, "Run, and join yourself to that chariot." Philip ran through the desert and joined himself to that chariot. There was a man that was an important official in the government of Ethiopia. Philip ran, and joined himself to that chariot, and won that man to Christ. God gave him strength to run. When you wait on the Lord, God gives you strength to run in the stressful times of life.

Staying Power

He says there will be staying power, "they will walk and not faint." It is one thing to soar like an eagle. It's another thing to run like an athlete. It's quite another thing just to be able to walk through the sorrows and sadness of life without fainting and giving up. To *walk* just means to live like a believer, to live the way that Jesus lived. To walk the way of the cross, to be able to walk the walk like you talk the talk. The Bible is teaching that if you wait on the Lord, if you exchange your weakness for His strength, if you exchange yourself for Him, so He's living His life through you, you'll be able to walk like Jesus walked. Everybody will be able to look at you and they'll see the difference. They'll see Jesus in your life and they'll know Jesus in the way that you live.

One of the saddest statements the Bible makes is found in Paul's epistle to the Ephesians, where he is describing those who do not have Christ. He says, "... they are without God and without hope in the world" *(Eph. 2:11)*. Honestly, I don't see how a person can survive without hope.

One of the hobbies I enjoy outside of pastoral ministry is fishing, especially offshore fishing. It is one of the many benefits of living on the Gulf Coast. Several years ago, my friend Vince and his brother Rob, and I went many miles off the coast in search of Snapper, Grouper, and Amberjack. The seas were a little rough that day. It wasn't long into the day when Rob began to turn green. If you have never been seasick, it is one of the worst feelings ever! The fish were really biting that day, so Vince made it clear we would NOT be heading back anytime soon. While Vince and I "hauled them in," Rob spent his time leaning over the rail. I felt so bad for Rob, but so glad for our fishing luck! After a while, in trying to encourage Rob, I patted him on the back and said, "Don't worry, brother, nobody's ever died of seasickness." Rob immediately responded, "Oh, don't tell me that! It's the hope of dying that keeps me going!"

You see, we can't live without hope! I have the hope that I'll see my loved ones again. I have the hope that one day, the earth is going to be filled with the glory of God, as waters cover the sea. I know that one of these days my hope will turn into reality and my faith will be sight. A man can't live without hope!

But there are those in this world without hope and without God! For true hope comes with God! Do you have hope? I mean, hope with a firm foundation, hope that is firmly based on the Word of God, hope that one day God will cleanse your life and make you the person He wants you to be. Hope that, you will see again those who have gone before you. The hope that the circle that is broken today will not remain broken because there will be a re-joining in the future! What a hope! Remember, "...we look not to the things that are seen but to the things that are unseen..." *(2 Corinthians 4:18)*

Chapter Three

LOVE

"Faith makes all things possible…
love makes all things easy."

- D.L. Moody

Therefore, since we have been justified by *faith*, we have peace with God through our Lord Jesus Christ. Through him we have also obtained access by faith into this grace in which we stand, and we rejoice in *hope* of the glory of God. Not only that, but we rejoice in our sufferings, knowing that suffering produces endurance, and endurance produces character, and character produces hope, and hope does not put us to shame, because God's *love* has been poured into our hearts through the Holy Spirit who has been given to us." (*Romans 5:1-5*)

Faith is *believing, trusting*. It is an assent of the mind to the truth God has revealed. And it is a submission to that truth in everyday life. Hope is "the confident expectation of something good." As stated earlier, in the Old Testament, words like *refuge* and *shelter* take the place of *hope*, meaning hope is the thing that protects us when everything else around us crumbles.

Love, contrary to popular thought, is not a feeling. Love is an attribute of God—He possessed it before He had someone with whom to show it. In the Old Testament, there are over 40 Hebrew words to describe God's love – that's how complex it is, and difficult to define. 1 John 4:8 says, "Anyone who does not love does not know God, because God is love." God's nature is love, for "God is love". Now that is not to say that love is God. You cannot reverse that statement. I have heard it put it this way, "Love does not define God, but God defines love." That is, all that God is and does is motivated by love. God created this world purely out of a motive of love. God created you and me just so He could love us. God created heaven so that He could have a place where we could love each other for all eternity. God desires that you know His great love.

"God's love has been poured into our hearts through the Holy Spirit . . ." (v.5). The word *into* speaks of being 'manifested.' The love of God has been poured out and manifested in our hearts. By the work of the Holy Spirit, the love of God has been made real in our hearts. Let's look at the love of God by first considering:

LOVE DEMONSTRATED

When we think about the love of God, we think about a love that is without question. A child may wonder if his or her parents love them and a spouse may question the love of a mate, but one need never doubt whether God loves them. God's love is certain and sure. His love is not without evidence, proof, and confirmation. You ask, "How can I know that God loves me?" Let me suggest two ways in which God has confirmed and demonstrated His love:

He Declared It

One reason we can know that God loves us is because He tells us He loves us. A wife might say to her husband, "If you love me, why don't you tell me?" In God's case, He repeatedly tells us in His Word that He loves. One such example is the familiar John 3:16: "For God so loved the world, that he gave his only Son, that whoever believes in him should not perish but have eternal life".

When you read John 3:16, read it as a personal word from God to you. Read it and listen to God saying, "I love you." But someone says, "I know God says He loves, but surely He is not saying that to me. After all I have done and how I have lived, He cannot be saying to me, 'I love you.'" Yet, I encourage you to read further and you will see that God says He "so loved the world." The word *world* removes any boundaries and embraces all nationalities. It is a word that takes in both Jews and Gentiles. It takes in the white man, black man, brown man, red man, and yellow man. It takes in all colors, classes, castes, and countries. It is a love that reaches into the icy huts of Greenland's mountains; to India's teeming multitude and the lonely jungles of Africa. Furthermore, 'world' is a word that lifts any restrictions and eliminates any conditions. In case someone might argue that when God spoke of loving the world, there are some in the world that were excluded.

Notice once again in John 3:16 and take note "whoever believes in Him should not perish." When God says that He loves "whoever"—that takes in everyone, including each of us, regardless of what we have done or who we are. It reaches to the civilized, but as well the savage. It reaches to the millionaire, but also to the pauper. It reaches to the strong, but also the weak. It reaches to the both the free and the slave. It is a love that also reaches behind every prison bar and even into the death cell where hardened criminals await their doom. It reaches into slums where men and women live in filth so vile that it would nauseate even the most hardened case worker, and even to the "red light" district where men and women's bodies have been ravaged by prostitution. It is a love that reaches to the highest, the grandest, and noblest, but also to the smallest, the lowest, and the meanest.

It is a love that not only reaches out to all colors, classes, castes, and countries, but also to all characters, all companies, and all conditions. It is as Romans 5:8 declares, "But God shows His love for us in that while we were still sinners, Christ died for us." It is a love that reaches to sinners, even the lowest and vilest of sinners.

When the great explorer Nansen was looking for the North Pole, each day he would let down the plummet to measure the depth of the ocean at a given point. One day he came to a place where the water was exceptionally deep. He dropped his line but it never reached bottom. He gathered up all the available rope on board the ship, attached it to the line, and still it did not reach bottom. In his report, Nansen wrote the exact length of the rope dropped, and then added the words, "Deeper than that."

As you read this, you may be wondering if God really loves you after all you have done. If I can answer it this way, God's love goes "deeper than that." It matters not how low you have fallen, no matter how deep you have sunk in the quagmire of sin, no matter the depths of your depravity, God's love goes deeper than that. How do we know that? He says so! He declared it!

He Displayed It

Once again look at John 3:16. We not only read, "For God so loved the world", but also that "He gave His only Son." If a person questions the love of God, look at the cross. There you see God's love proven and demonstrated. We read in 1 John 3:16, "By this we know love, that he laid down his life for us, and we ought to lay down our lives for the brothers." We also read in 1 John 4:9, "In this the love of God was made manifest among us, that God sent his only Son into the world, so that we might live through him." I remind you that we do not measure the love of God by how good life is or whether or not we are healthy and wealthy. We measure the love of God by the gift of His Son who died on the cross for our sins. It is there we see the proof and evidence of His love. If you want to know if God really loves us, go to the cross. John R. Rice put it this way in his work, *The Sword Book of Treasures*:

"Go to the top of the cross and write, 'The height of God's love.' Stoop beneath the nail-pierced feet that never touched nor walked in sin, and write, 'The depth of God's love.' Then walk around to the left of the cross, the side where the heart of God beats, the heart that bore our griefs and sorrows, the heart that wept over the lost condition of sinners, and at the fingertips of that bruised and bleeding hand, write, 'The length of God's love.' And then walk around to the opposite side, the right hand, the everlasting hand, the hand that cradled the universe, the hand that was dipped into the sea of eternity to form the worlds, the hand that blessed the little children, the hand that lifted up the woman taken in adultery, the hand that rebuked the winds and waves. Go there and write, 'The breadth of God's love.'"

The song says it well:

> *Could we with ink the ocean fill,*
> *And were the skies of parchment made;*
> *Were every stalk on earth a quill,*
> *And every man a scribe by trade;*
> *To write the love of God above,*
> *Would drain the ocean dry;*
> *Nor could the scroll contain the whole,*
> *Though stretched from sky to sky.*

The best expression and example of God's love is the cross where Jesus died for our sins. There at the cross, Jesus died for every sinner and paid the price for every vile sin imaginable. There is the proof of God's love. There is the evidence of God's love. There we see the love of God demonstrated!

What am I saying? I am saying that no matter who you are or what you have done, God loves you. It is a love demonstrated by His Words.

LOVE DESCRIBED

If it is not thrilling enough to know that God loves us, to understand and realize that there is no end to His love leaves us standing in awe. It is not just that God loves, but also that He will always love us. The Bible describes how there can be:

No Separation from His Love

The question is asked in Romans 8:35, "Who shall separate us from the love of Christ?" The answer is given in verses 38-39, "For I am sure that neither death nor life, nor angels nor rulers, nor things present nor things to come, nor powers, nor height nor depth, nor anything else in all creation, will be able to separate us from the love of God in Christ Jesus our Lord."

It is not just that God loves us, but that He will always love us.

What is God saying to us? He is telling us there is nothing around us or above us that can separate us from the love of God. There is nothing below us, behind us, or before us that can separate us from His love. There is nothing we can experience or encounter that can separate us from the love of God. There is no fear or fate that can separate us from the love of God. In other words, God's love does not depend on anything or anyone. He will always love us. Yes, we will falter and fail, but He will always love us. Yes, we will stumble and sin, but He will still love us. We must understand that God hates sin and will judge all unconfessed sin, yet even when we sin, He does not cease to love us. Nothing, absolutely nothing, shall or can separate us from the love of God.

No Stopping of His Love

Nothing can separate us from God's love. Furthermore, there will never be a moment when God will not love us. Listen to what God told Jeremiah in Jeremiah 31:3: "I have loved you with an everlasting love."

> *We are to guard our heart, to ensure that the reality of God's love continues to be a force in our life.*

Since God is an everlasting God, His love can be nothing but an everlasting love. I love the words of Robert L. Moyer in his book *John 3:16*:

"You may go back beyond the time when a wave beat upon the beach, or a star shone in the sky, or the leaf of a tree fluttered in the breeze, and an angel worshipped before the throne, and when you can get back as far as the mind can reach, you will be no nearer the beginning of God's love for you than you are now. If you project your mind into the future to the time when the mountains have molded down into the dust, or out beyond the time when the sun has grown cold, and the stars are old, and the leaves of the judgment book unfold, you will be no nearer the end of God's love than you are now."

There is no question that God loved us when He gave His Son to die for our sins on the cross. Yet, I remind you that He loves you as much today as He did then. He will always love you with the same kind of love He displayed at Calvary. His love is an everlasting love.

LOVE DEFENDED

There is one final verse we need to examine regarding God's love for us. It is found in verse 21 of the little book of Jude: "Keep yourselves in the love of God, waiting for the mercy of our Lord Jesus Christ that leads to eternal life." We are told to keep ourselves in the love of God. Does this mean that I have to live a certain way or do certain things to keep God loving me? Considering that we just saw that God's love is an everlasting love, obviously not. What then is the Bible saying to me when it tells me to keep myself in the love of God? The word, 'keep' means, "to watch, to defend, and guard from injury or loss by properly keeping the eye upon." We are to guard our heart, to ensure that the reality of God's love continues to be a force in our life.

How then can we keep ourselves in the love of God? I believe that the instruction of Jude involves thinking about God's love. In other words, I am to constantly think about the love of God. It is a subject that I am to think about on a continuous basis so that the love of God is constantly moving and stirring me. Why should we spend so much time thinking about the love of God? Let me suggest two reasons:

The Awareness of God's Love

We are to think constantly about God's love so that we never forget that He loves us. Life is not always easy. We can find ourselves facing very dark times, but it is a great comfort and strength to know that He loves us. No matter what you are going through or may go through, never forget God loves you. The second reason I suggest why we should constantly think about the love of God is:

The Appreciation for God's Love

Why are you saved? Are you saved because of the kind of life you have lived? Are you saved because you built up a necklace of prayer beads that hangs to the floor or because you lived a good outstanding religious and moral life? No! We are saved because God loved us enough to give his only begotten Son to die for our sins on the cross. If God had not loved us, we would be eternally lost without an ounce of hope of being saved.

On September 22, 1993, the worst train crash in Amtrak history occurred just north of where I live (Mobile, Alabama). The Amtrak Sunset Limited plunged into the Conner Creek Bayou a few minutes after three o'clock in the morning. Survivors described a combination of explosion, fire, falling, and being thrown under water. Unknown to those on the train, a tugboat pushing a barge had slammed into the train bridge that crossed the bayou. In the darkness no one could see the extent of the damage. Unaware of what had happened, the train crossed the bridge at 70 m.p.h. There were 210 passengers on board. As the train crossed the damaged support, its weight caused the bridge to give away. Three locomotive units and the first four of the train's eight passenger cars fell into the alligator infested bayou. Within seconds, a large orange fireball engulfed the area, presumably, one of the locomotives exploding. The tugboat operator immediately called in a frantic message to the Coast Guard. But it was so far back, that emergency vehicles were only able to get within six miles of the site on land. Helicopters had to be called in to help with the rescue. The helicopters were hampered in their rescue by an extremely dark night, and the skies filled with dense smoke created by burning diesel fuel. To add to the problems, there was no place to land their helicopters. It was forty to forty-five minutes before anyone could get to the scene to begin rescue efforts. Forty-seven people died either from drowning or by burning to death, but there would have been many more if it had not been for many heroes in those early morning hours. Passengers helped each other by forming lines and passing people, hand-to-hand, to the shore. There was Michael Dopheide, a 26-year old law school graduate that helped dozens of people from the submerged cars. He coaxed people to jump from the train into the water and helped them to a metal girder until they could be rescued. In all he helped save the lives of thirty people, including a two-year old child and an eleven-year-old girl with cerebral palsy named Andrea.

It is the story of Andrea and her parents, Geary and Mary Jane Chancey, that paints a beautiful picture of this kind of love. They were traveling home when the accident happened. They were trying to get out, when the car they were in shifted and suddenly filled with water. In a final desperate act, they pushed little Andrea through a window into the arms of Michael Dopheide. It was their last act of love for their daughter. Instead of trying to save their own lives, they chose to save their daughter.

Why should we keep ourselves in the love of God? It is because the Lord chose to give His life so that we all might live. It was the greatest act of love this world has ever known. It is a love that ought to be deeply appreciated by each of us and never forgotten. We would not be saved, if not for the love of God that gave the Lord Jesus to die for us. We have a wonderful God and He is no greater than in His love!

SECTION 2

AMPLIFY

Chapter Four

PASSION

"Get on fire for God and men will come and see you burn."
- John Wesley

Up to this point, we have attempted to SIMPLIFY *Faith*, *Hope*, and *Love*: what it is, where it comes from, and how to receive them. But what do these look like AMPLIFIED in our life?

To begin with, what does Faith look like amplified in your life? One word: PASSION. Why do we need it, and why should we want it? Because it is nearly impossible to stop passion! Passion will plow through, jump over, or dig under its obstacles. Passion is the fuel in your engine. Big engines can be rendered useless without fuel. Passion is food for the soul. It's passion that which sets you apart from others. Passion is the secret of life.

Life, at its very best, is a passionate experience, not a doctoral dissertation. In Jesus Christ, more than anyone else, He shows us what it means to live with passion. In fact, He expects us to live with passion. Listen to the words of our Lord Jesus: "So, because you are lukewarm, and neither hot nor cold, I will spit you out of my mouth." *(Rev. 3:16)*. Jesus did not invite lukewarm faith. The gospel was not meant to be comfortable or safe. Instead, God promises to spit the lukewarm out of His mouth. Faith should be passionate, not lukewarm.

The spiritual life, the *FAITH* life, is meant to be the passionate life. The life of faith is a life spent following Jesus, and Jesus is not a two-dimensional make-believe deity who does our bidding. He leads us into an all-consuming experience of life!

PASSION DEFICIENT

Are you lacking passion today? Why does anyone lack passion? Let me suggest a few reasons I believe people can become passion-deficient.

The Precious Becomes Familiar

It can be your spouse, children, even your relationship with God: The precious can become familiar. Max Lucado calls it "the poison of the ordinary." That which once was special, extraordinary, is now ordinary, common. In *God Came Near*, Lucado writes about what he calls 'the agent of familiarity: to take everything for granted.

> "The Enemy's goal is nothing less than to take what is most precious to us and make it appear most common. He's an expert in robbing the sparkle and replacing it with the drab. He invented

the yawn and put the hum in the humdrum. And his strategy is deceptive. He won't steal your salvation; he'll just make you forget what it was like to be lost. You'll grow accustomed to prayer and thereby not pray. Worship will become commonplace and study optional. With the passing of time he'll infiltrate your heart with boredom and cover the cross with dust so you'll be "safely" out of reach of change. Score one for the agent of familiarity. Nor will he steal your home from you; he'll do something far worse. He'll paint it with a familiar coat of drabness. He'll replace evening gowns with bathrobes, nights on the town with evenings in the recliner, and romance with routine. He'll scatter the dust of yesterday over the wedding pictures in the hallway until they become a memory of another couple in another time. He won't take your children, he'll just make you too busy to notice them. His whispers to procrastinate are seductive. There is always next summer to coach the team, next month to go to the lake, and next week to teach Johnny how to pray. He'll make you forget that the faces around your table will soon be at tables of their own. Hence, books will go unread, games will go unplayed, hearts will go unnurtured, and opportunities will go ignored. All because the poison of the ordinary has deadened your senses to the magic of the moment. Before you know it, the little face that brought tears to your eyes in the delivery room has become—perish the thought—common. A common kid sitting in the back seat of your van as you whiz down the fast lane of life. Unless something changes, unless someone wakes you up, that common kid will become a common stranger."

Acceptance and Approval

We want to be accepted by others and want their approval. But passion both repels people and draws people all at the same time. It may be our tendency to turn down the heat of passion in order to seek to be normal, average – like other people.

Our Society is Passive

We live in a very passive society. We become like our environment. As we watch the news, we see the trend of becoming more like our culture.

Apathy Tends to Increase with Age

It's a fact that, as we grow older, our enthusiasm and passion tend to decrease. Researchers have determined that as we age, our brain actually shrinks. And apathy is linked to lower brain volume.

No Purpose Beyond Ourselves

Many live today with no purpose beyond themselves. We live in a culture that drives the "looking out for number one" mindset. But the truth is, as John Maxwell puts it, "People who live for themselves are in a mighty small business."

PASSION DESCRIBED

Let me give you a working definition for passion: Passion is "an unquenchable, all-consuming desire." As a Christ-follower, what do I need to know about passion?

Passion Changes Lives

In 2 Corinthians 9:2, Paul writes, "for I know your readiness, of which I boast about you to the people of Macedonia, saying that Achaia has been ready since last year. And your zeal has stirred up most of them." We can say with confidence, that passion changes the lives of others.

One example is Robert Murray McCheyne, one of Scotland's greatest preachers, who died when he was only twenty-nine years old. A biographer wrote that everywhere he stepped, Scotland shook. Whenever he opened his mouth, a spiritual force seemed to sweep in every direction. Thousands followed him to the feet of Christ. A traveler, eager to see where McCheyne had preached, went to his old church. An old sexton agreed to give him a tour. He led the way into McCheyne's study. "Sit in that chair," he ordered. The traveller hesitated a moment, then sat in the chair. On the table before him was an open Bible. "Drop your head in that book and weep. That is what our minister always did before he preached," said the old man. He then led the visitor into the pulpit before another open Bible. "Stand there," he said, "and drop your head on your hands and let the tears flow. That is the way our minister always conducted himself before he began to preach!" With such a passion for God's Word and the souls of the lost, is it any wonder the Holy Spirit used McCheyne to draw so many to the Savior?

Passion also changes *me*. Passion will change your priorities. Passion will change your goals. Passion will change how you view and live each day! If you follow your passion, instead of others' perceptions, you cannot help but become a more dedicated, productive person. And that increases your ability to impact others. In the end, your passion will have more influence than your personality.

Passion Makes Impossibilities Possible

Passion eliminates certain words from your vocabulary. Words like: *retreat, compromise, half-hearted, giving up.* Those concepts cease to be options for you. The key to willpower is "wantpower." People who want something badly enough can usually find the willpower to achieve it. Human beings are so made that whenever anything fires up the soul, impossibilities vanish.

Passion Helps Protect You from Wrong

Passionate focus keeps you from taking a detour. You are driven, one way, His way. With passionate faith comes a great desire for personal holiness. We will talk more about this in the next chapter, when we describe HOPE amplified.

PASSION DERIVED

How do I obtain passion? How do I possess it? In my study of passion, I have discovered some things I believe increase passion in a believer's life. Below are some suggestions:

Believe Passion Makes a Difference

Passion can be the deciding difference in your life. Paul writes in Romans 12:11, "Do not be slothful in zeal, be fervent in spirit, serve the Lord." If you look at the lives of effective leaders, you find they often don't fit into a stereotypical mold. For example, more than 50 percent of all CEO's of Fortune 500 companies had C or C- averages in college. Nearly 75 percent of all U.S. presidents were in the bottom half of their school classes. And more than 50 percent of all millionaire entrepreneurs never finished college. What makes it possible for people who might seem ordinary to achieve great things? The answer is passion! It has been said, "The difference between a successful person and others is not a lack of strength, not a lack of knowledge, but rather a lack of passion."

Realize God Desires Passionate Christians
Titus 2:14 says, "who gave himself for us to redeem us from all lawlessnes and to purify for himself a people that are his own possession who are zealous for good works." We are not only to approve of good works, and speak for good works, but we are to be red-hot for them. We are to be on fire for everything that is right and true. We may no be content with being quiet and inoffensive, but oassionate about good works in serving our Lord.

Pray for Passion
One of my most significant prayers morning after morning is simply this: that God would give me a passion for the life I'm living and for Him. Sometimes it's just hard to face another day of the same old thing. I heard about an old country preacher who prayed:

"Okay Lord, give me this mornin' the eyes of the eagle and wisdom of the owl. Illuminate my brow with the sun of heaven. Possess my mind with the love for the people. Turpentine my imagination, grease my lips, electrify my brain with the lightin' of the Word. Fill me plumb full of the dynamite of Your glory, anoint me all over with the kerosene of salvation, and set me on fire. Amen."

Return to Your First Love

Apathy isn't a just a state of the mind, it's a state of the heart. 'Apathy' means to have no passion. Jesus accused the church in Ephesus of losing their passion. In Revelation 2:2-5, He says:

> "I know your works, your toil and your patient endurance, and how you cannot bear with those who are evil, but have tested those who call themselves apostles and are not, and found them to be false. I know you are enduring patiently and bearing up for my name's sake, and you have not grown weary. But I have this against you, that you have abandoned the love you had at first. Remember therefore from where you have fallen; repent, and do the works you did at first. If not, I will come to you and remove your lampstand from its place, unless you repent."

So, according to His instructions, we are to first "repent" of our apathy. Then, we are to "remember." Remember what? Remember what it used to be like, when you were passionately on fire for Christ. In addition, remember all that God has done for you. Finally, we are to "do the works you did at first." In other words, "Re-do." Have you lost your zeal, your passion? Repent, Remember, and Re-do!

Activate Your Spiritual Gifts

If we want to increase our passion we need to release our gifts. We all have spiritual gifts, even though we may not have used them yet. It is like when your baby teeth came in. Behind those baby teeth are another set of teeth that will emerge at an appointed time. We can activate our gifts just my walking by faith. If you have a burden for the sick, go to the hospital and start praying for people. Be willing to serve and minister to others. As a result, you will begin to see those gifts manifest and your passion increase.

Associate with People with Passion

Passion is contagious. The biggest single predictor of success (however you want to define it) is the people who surround you. As discussed earlier, the world influences us more than we realize, and more than we'd like to believe. Think of the five or ten people you spend the most time with. What are these people doing? How passionate are they? Do they inspire you? If the answer is no, then it's time to find new friends. I've determined in my own life not to spend much of my time with negative people.

Stories

I am inspired by other's stories. I often read biographies. Everyone out there has had days when they lose all self-confidence and feel like they are going nowhere. All your ideas start sounding stupid and you don't know why you're still trying in the first place. This is where these inspirational biographies come into play. People who have held on to their ideas and passions and executed them regardless of how difficult it was to keep going. By reading some of these stories, you will recognize exactly where your passions lie and figure out just what you need to keep doing to make them happen. As I read or hear these stories I think, "Well, if God did that that there for them, He can do it here, in me, as well."

Will you pray for passion today? If you are passion deficient, will you repent, remember, and take action? Remember, Faith AMPLIFIED in a believer's life is ***purposeful passion!***

Chapter Five

PURITY

"Holiness, not happiness, is the chief end of man."

- Oswald Chambers

As we discussed in Chapter 2, *Hope* is "the confident expectation of something good." For the believer that "something good" is the Second Coming; the future meeting with Christ. We are waiting, hoping for His return. Expectant waiting for someone changes us. Can you remember how you waited, perhaps, at an airport for someone you longed to meet again? The Bible teaches that the hope of our future meeting with Christ will begin to change us now. "And everyone who thus HOPES in Him purifies himself as He is pure." *(I John 3:3)*

What does HOPE look like amplified in a believer's

life? Lived out fully? Hope amplified is PURITY. The Bible also calls it "holiness" and "sanctification."

You see, Jesus *is* pure, and therefore, we want to *be* pure when we come into His presence. This doesn't mean that we can remove all sin from our lives. It does mean that because we know Christ as our Lord and Savior, we are allowing the Holy Spirit to make us more and more like Him. "And we all, with unveiled face, beholding the glory of the Lord, are being transformed into the same image from one degree of glory to another. For this comes from the Lord who is the Spirit." *(2 Cor. 3:18)* One way to find out if you truly believe in Jesus is to ask yourself if you're seriously interested in becoming more like Him. Are you? And if you are, what are you doing about it?

THE DESCRIPTION

PURITY, or holiness, means "set apart" in some special and exclusive way. In Holy Matrimony, for example, a man and a woman are set apart, leaving all others as they bond exclusively with each other. We are set apart unto the Lord. That means making a decisive break from sin. The Bible says in 1 John 3:6, "No one who abides in him keeps on sinning; no one who keeps on sinning has either seen him or known him." You see, sin breaks our relationship with God. Sin silences our prayer life. Sin keeps us from worship. Sin causes us to withdraw from fellowship with other Christians. Sin isolates us. Purity, on the other hand, does just the opposite. It keeps us close to God and close to others who are close to God.

Purity is powerful. Purity can hold you together even when your life feels like it's out of control. Purity opens your eyes and ears to the truth. Purity enables you to see past deceit and deception. When we have pure hearts, we can see the presence of God. I want you to notice that the Scripture links purity to hope. 1 John 3:3 is the key verse, let's look at it again: "And everyone who thus hopes in him [Christ] purifies himself as he [Jesus Christ] is pure."

The connection of purity and hope is important because we often link purity to fear. We think we better keep our lives pure because God is going to punish us if we don't. We think that punishment might be a disease like cancer, or the death of a loved one, or the fires of hell. I've not found, however, that people become pure when they are motivated by fear, not even the fear of God's punishment. That's because trying to escape punishment is a self-centered motivation. But that is not the teaching of the Bible. In fact, it teaches the opposite. We don't move toward God out of fear,

> **The three "Ds" of spiritual breakdown are defeat, damage, and depression.**

but with hope. It's our eagerness to see Christ, and our hope in His coming again that motivates us to rid ourselves of everything that is unworthy of His love for us. We know that we matter to Him—He died on the cross to show us His love for us. And we want to offer Him the purest life we can.

This is why people who lose hope are also likely to lose their commitment to purity. The three "Ds" of spiritual breakdown are defeat, damage, and depression. Those who live defeated, damaged, and depressed lives usually see no point to keeping themselves pure. "Why not indulge in that drink? Why not say that lie? Why not break my promise? Why not transgress that commandment? Why not compromise my morals? Why not ... when I don't think my life matters that much anymore?" But God says otherwise: "See what kind of love the Father has given to us, that we should be called children of God . . ." (*1 John 3:1a*)

And there's more: "Beloved, we are God's children now, and what we willbe has not yet appeared; but we know that when he [Christ] appears,we shall be like him, because we shall see him as he is." (*1 John 3:2*)

God does not abandon His children. When you come to Christ in faith you become a son or daughter of God. God will never turn away from you. He has a future for you, and that future will not be finally revealed until Christ returns. That is HOPE! That is OUR HOPE! We don't know everything about that future, but we do know that we will be like Christ, because we will see Him as He is in all His purity, glory, and love. "Beloved, we are God's children. . ."

I was at a conference several years ago where everyone picked up a "Hello My Name Is" tag as they entered the room. With available black markers we were to write our names and adhere it to our clothing. During a break I found myself next to a woman whose name tag read "Beloved." I was intrigued by the name. I wanted to know that woman's story. So I turned to her and said, "I've been noticing your name, 'Beloved.' It's a beautiful name. Please tell me about how it was chosen for you." "Oh, my name is Tina," the woman explained, "but I've always wanted someone to call me 'Beloved.' So when I came to this conference I decided to give myself that name. I wanted a full day of hearing people tell me that I'm loved."

We don't have to pretend that our name is "Beloved." It's right here in the Scripture. It's the name given to every one who comes to God through Jesus Christ. We are His beloved children!

THE DESIRE

As beloved children we should desire purity. The Apostle Peter tells us in 1 Peter 1:14-16, "As obedient children, do not be conformed to the passions of your former ignorance, but as he who called you is holy, you also be holy in all your conduct, since it is written, 'You shall be holy, for I am holy.'"

Are you an obedient child? There are three basic reasons for obedience: A slave obeys because he *has* too. An employee obeys because he *needs* too. A loving child obeys because he *wants* to . . . he desires it. One proof that you are saved is that you obey His Word because you want to! In 1 Peter 1:2 we read, "according to the foreknowledge of God the Father, in the sanctification of the Spirit, for obedience . . ." I don't strive to obey God's Word because I have to or because I need to, I strive to obey it because I want to! Jesus says in John 14:15, "if you love me, you will keep my commandments." Do you know why holiness/purity is revealed in the character of the child of God? It's because we're His children! You've heard the expression: "like father, like son?" That is what Peter is talking about here. Because we are His children, there is His likeness in our lives—and His likeness is holiness! "Be holy, for I am holy."

THE DEMAND

Holiness should be our desire, but it is also His DEMAND. We read further in 1 Peter 1:16-17, "since it is written, 'You shall be holy, for I am holy.' And if you call on him as Father who judges impartially according to each one's deeds, conduct yourselves with fear throughout the time of your exile."

Now we know that God is love, we know that God is power, we know that God is light, but God is also holy. "Holy, holy, holy, is the Lord God of Hosts." God's prime attribute is holiness, and so as His obedient beloved children we are to pursue purity, to walk in holiness.

The word "judges" there is a very interesting word. It does not mean to judge in the sense of condemnation. He is not saying God is trying to condemn you. The Bible says "those who know Christ have passed from death unto life." And the Bible says, "there is therefore no condemnation for them who are in Christ Jesus." Well, what does it mean that God judges us? It means to judge with the view of finding something worthy in you that He might bless you or reward you. Do you know why God is watching every thing you do? God loves you so much, God cares for you so much, you are His child, that God is just excited when He can find obedience, holiness in you, dedication in you. It gives Him an occasion to reward and to bless your life.

That is exciting, isn't it? God examines us. That is one of the reasons we should live a holy life, because our Father does not want to be disappointed in us. Our Father does not want to condemn us, He wants to bless our life. And so this judgment is a family judgment. That makes me feel good, because as I look at my child, I don't look at my child to find things I might criticize. I watch my child and I am always thrilled and pleased when I find obedience in my child.

Not long after my son Christopher began driving, a church member came up to me on a Sunday after services and in a very gruff manner asked, "Who taught your son how to drive?" To be honest, I was tempted to say, "his mom." But I didn't, and told him it was me who taught him. The man then began to say that he happened to follow my son to church as he left our neighborhood that morning. He then began to describe how good Christopher was as a young driver, fully stopping at the stop signs, proper use of turn signals, and never exceeded the speed limit. I was both relieved and proud!

You fathers and mothers know how it thrills your heart. And so it is good to know that not only is our Father a judge, but the judge is our Father.

THE DYNAMIC

God never makes a demand without providing the dynamic, the process by which we are made holy and pure. The Biblical word for this process is sanctification. "And because of him you are in Christ Jesus, who became to us wisdom from God, righteousness and sanctification and redemption." *(1 Cor. 1:30)*

This simply means that God makes holiness available to us by the incoming and indwelling life of the Lord Jesus.

Peter tells us in 2 Pet. 1:4:

> "by which he has granted to us his precious and very great promises, so that through them you may become partakers of the divine nature, having escaped from the corruption that is in the world because of sinful desire."

The holiness that Jesus preached, practiced, and purchased is imparted to believers. Thus, we are partakers of the Divine Nature. In other words, when WE do OUR part, HE does HIS part. His part is sanctification, holiness and FRUIT. "But now that you have been set free from sin and have become slaves of God, the fruit you get leads to sanctification (*holiness*) and its end, eternal life." *(Romans 6:22)*

Fruitfulness from God

What does the Bible mean when it talks about fruitfulness? Let me give you a definition of fruit. Fruit is the outward expression of the inner nature. If I see an apple hanging from a tree, I assume that it is an apple tree. I see an orange hanging from a tree, and I know that's an orange tree. I see spaghetti hanging from a tree, and I say, that's a spaghetti tree! Now some people can tell what kind of tree it is by looking at the leaf, or at the bark. I can't. I have to see the outward manifestation. I have to see the fruit. So, fruit is the outward manifestation of the inner nature. What is our inward nature? It is Christ himself. And by the way, over in Galatians 5 Paul tells us what a fruitful saint looks like in verses 22-23. That's what He does for us, through us, is bear fruit. So the question, therefore, is . . . what is OUR part? I John 3:3 tells us, "And everyone who thus hopes in him purifies himself as he is pure." What does it mean to "purify yourself?"

Yieldedness to God

"Just as you used to offer the parts of your body in slavery to impurity and to ever-increasing wickedness, so now offer them in slavery to righteousness leading to holiness" *(Romans 6:19b NIV)*. Jesus said in John 15:5, "I am the vine; you are the branches. Whoever abides in me and I in him, he it is that bears much fruit, for apart from me you can do nothing." Notice the branches don't produce the fruit. They bear the fruit. It is the vine that produces the fruit. The branch is just a "grape rack" that God has there to hang His fruit on. The branch can do nothing of itself. Jesus said, "without me you can do nothing." It is the Lord Jesus who produces the fruit. I simply bear it. What this means is that if I am going to be a fruitful Christian, I need to live the life of a branch. That's it. Live the life of a branch. Abide in Jesus. My fruitfulness comes simply by being available to help and by resting in Him, knowing that will happen as He lives in me, and I keep up this vital communion and union with Jesus Christ. All I have to do is to make certain that the life of Jesus, the Holy Spirit's fullness, is flowing unhindered through my life. You know what? He'll push off the old dead leaves of hate, pride, jealousy; and He'll push on the new fruit of love, joy, patience.

Yieldedness precedes fruitfulness. A believer who is living a life of practical holiness will know what it is to be completely and continually yielded to God. Such yieldedness implies a once-for-all act of surrender followed by a daily attitude of surrender. Our motto becomes, "not I, but Christ." Jesus is enough. I am to pray, "Lord, you are enough" regardless of the situation in my life: marriage, finances, temptation, etc. This is what Jesus meant in John 15:5, 'without me, you can do nothing."

> "For the grace of God has appeared, bringing salvation for all people, training us to renounce ungodliness and worldly passions, and to live self-controlled, upright, and godly lives in the present age, waiting for our blessed hope, the appearing of the glory of our great God and Savior Jesus Christ." *(Titus 2:11-13)*

Knowing that Jesus is coming motivates us to be holy. Jesus is coming and knowing that He is...we need to be holy. Be holy! Be set apart! Let others see Jesus in you, so that when He comes,

> "with trumpet sound,
> oh may I then in Him be found,
> dressed in his righteousness alone,
> faultless, holy, to stand before the throne."

Be holy so that the world can see us and say, "Wow, what a God!" What your neighbors see in you, what your coworkers see in you, what your fellow students see in you is what they come to believe about God. "Be holy, for I am holy."

Chapter Six

OUR PURPOSE

"Whatever a person may be like, we must still love them because we love God."

- John Calvin

We are greatly loved by God, and He has poured out His love into our hearts by His Holy Spirit. I want to now show you in this chapter that God wants YOU to live out that love; for it is your life's PURPOSE. I have found that many people wonder what their purpose is.

Mike Royco reported this true story in the *Chicago Tribune*. "A man named Bill Mallory traveled to India to discover the purpose of life. But he didn't find the answer there. So after returning, he noticed a sign at a Chevron gas station that simply said, 'As you travel, ask us.' So every time he pulled into a Chevron station, he would look to the sign and say, 'I'm a traveler. I'd like to ask you a question. What is the purpose of life?' These were the real answers he got. I'm not making this up. The first guy said, 'Sorry, I'm new here.' The second guy said, 'I don't remember anything in the manual about that.' Another guy said, 'I'm not much for church myself, sir.' One guy gave him a leering look and a wink, whatever that meant. However, most people just gave him a blank stare, cleaned his windshield; but he kept asking at all the Chevron stations. One day Mallory got a phone call from Chevron Customer Relations. He said, 'We understand you've been asking our dealer questions and getting unsatisfactory answers.' The man suggested that he write out his question and send it to Chevron Corporate with a self-addressed stamped envelope. So Bill Mallory wrote, 'What is the purpose of life?' and sent it to Chevron Gas Company. A couple of weeks later, the envelope was returned. The only thing in it was an application for a credit card!"

Matthew 22:37-40 teaches that our purpose, in light of His great love for us, is to love Him back; and to love others. "And he said to him, 'You shall love the Lord your God with all your heart and with all your soul and with all your mind. This is the great and first commandment. And a second is like it: You shall love your neighbor as yourself. On these two commandments depend all the Law and the Prophets.'"

LOVING GOD

Jesus said in v37, "You shall love the Lord your God . . ." Think of how God desires our love. Hosea 6:6 says, "For I desire steadfast love and not sacrifice, the knowledge of God rather than burnt offerings." God wants you to know Him and love Him. God doesn't want ritual, religion, rules, and regulations; He wants a relationship. God wants us to love Him. Furthermore He deserves our love. Why would we not love Him? But the words "You shall" force us to consider loving God from an altogether different perspective. He demands our love. We are commanded to "love the Lord your God."

Jesus not only desires, deserves, and demands our love for God, but He also describes that love by saying that we are to love the Lord our God, "with all your heart and with all your soul and with all your mind." Every Jew recognized that statement as part of the *Shema*, the basic and essential creed of Judaism. It was actually a quote from Deuteronomy 6:5. It was the sentence by which every Jewish service opened then and still opens now. It was the first text that every Jewish child committed to memory. Jesus was describing the most basic and fundamental truth of our relationship with God: that we are to love Him with all our heart, soul, and mind. What kind of love is Jesus describing?

> *God doesn't want ritual, religion, rules, or regulations; He wants a relationship.*

The Totality

Consider the totality of this love for God. It was a call for total love, full love, and a complete love for God. The little word "all" that Jesus used three times speaks of a total love. It describes that which is, "complete, whole, every whit, altogether." We might use the term, "our whole being." The love that Jesus described is not a half-hearted love.

I think of the fellow who said to his girl friend, "Darling, I love you. I'd climb the highest mountain for you; I'd swim the deepest stream for you; I'd fight a jungle of lions for you; and if it doesn't rain tonight, I'll be over to see you." That's not the kind of love Jesus described. He was speaking of loving God with our whole being. It is loving Him with every fiber of our being. It is a total love.

The Personality

There is also the personality of this love for God. Jesus described the personality of this love. First, we are to love God with "all your heart." Jesus was speaking of the emotional side of this love. The heart is the seat of emotions. Jesus was saying that our love for God has an emotional personality. Love is an emotional thing. If you have ever fallen in love you know what I am talking about. There are those "feelings" that are associated with love. Our love for God is not to be without feelings or emotions. There should not be an absence of feelings and emotions in our love for God. Instead, we should love God so much that we are emotionally affected.

I think about when we come to church. I know there are some who would have you to believe that you are to bundle up your emotions and feelings and leave them in the car when you get to church. Under the premise of "reverence" all emotions are to be divorced from the service and our worship. You will have to forgive me, but I can't be that way. God has been too good and done too much for me. When someone gets to singing, talking, and preaching about Jesus, the cross, God's love for me, God's saving grace, I get emotional. Why? Because I love Him with all my heart.

Jesus also said that we are to love God with "all your soul." Jesus was speaking of not only the emotional, but also the spiritual side of this love. The word "soul" speaks of the spirit, the part of man that communes with God and relates to God. To love God in the fashion Jesus described affects us spiritually. When we love God with all our soul we will make Him Lord.

Another characteristic of this love is that we are to love God with "all your mind." There is the emotional and spiritual side of this love, but there is also the mental side of this love. When you really love someone you think about him or her constantly. They are in your thoughts all through the day. Through the years, my ministry has consisted of being gone from home quite a bit. It has been my habit to try to call or text home every night between 9:00 and 10:00 p.m., even when I am out of the country. If I don't get to talk to Kathy, it is hard for me to sleep. Why? No matter what I have to do during the day, she is always on my mind. I think about her all the time. Kathy will tell you that I text her 5-10 times a day. When I see certain things and go certain places, I am thinking, "I wish Kathy could see this or be here." You could say that I am preoccupied with her. I am not exaggerating when I say she is always on my mind. Let me say it this way, when we love God as we should love Him, He will always be on our mind. You are constantly thinking about Him. Why? You are in love with Him.

There is a final characteristic that I want you to see. In Mark 12:30 we read, "And with all strength." You see, there is the physical side of this love. This is the practical expression of love. "Whatever you do, work at it with all your heart, as working for the Lord, not for human masters." *(Colossians 3:23 NIV)*

If you get this verse, it will absolutely change your life. It helps you to understand that in order to worship God, you don't have to change jobs, you just change who you're working for. When you change who you're working for, your work becomes worship. Worship is an expression of your love for God. Many compartmentalize their lives. God says, "I want you to invite me into every area of your life. I want to be involved in all of it." Get this truth: In life, it's not *what* you do that matters; it is *who* you do it for. You give it all to God. All of your work can be turned to worship. It does not matter if you're a butcher, a baker, or a candlestick maker. You can do it for God. You may be a carpet cleaner, an attorney, or a nurse. You may be a mother raising children, an executive, sales person, or a truck driver. It really doesn't matter what you do. It's who you do it for. This turns your *work* into *worship*. God doesn't want worship to just be a church thing. He wants it to be your whole life. He wants you to worship God with your life. We will serve Him, follow Him, obey Him, and live for Him. I am often asked, "How do you get people to work?" My answer is very simple. Get them to love God. If people love God with all their soul and strength then they will serve and work for God.

Do you love the Lord as Jesus described? Do you love Him with all your heart, with all your soul, with all your mind, and with all your strength? That's how God wants to be loved!

LOVING OTHERS

Jesus goes on in the text that describes our purpose by saying in Matthew 22:38-39, "And he said to him, 'This is the great and first commandment. And a second is like it: You shall love your neighbor as yourself.'" Are you surprised that the two are related, loving God and loving others? In fact, they are inseparably connected. You see, the more we love God, the more we love people. The higher the temperature of our love for God rises, the higher the temperature for the love of people rises. And by the way, God didn't pick and choose; He loves them all. And that has to be true with us also.

Is loving people that important? Well, out of the all the commandments, Jesus says this is the most important. Out of all the things that Jesus asks us to do, this is the most important. Without hesitation, Jesus said, "You shall love your neighbor as yourself." You see, love is the greatest value. If you want to know what God values most – it's love. It is the greatest thing that we can do. Now I think that is because loving people is so hard. Have you noticed that? Loving some people is difficult. And there are irregular people out there, even a few jerks and jerkettes. But we are to love all of them, and that's hard at times. In fact, we can't do that on our own. And that may be why fifty-five times in the New Testament, we're commanded to love. If God says something one time, it is important, but if He says it three times we better listen up—it's really, really, really important. But with love, God doesn't just say it, He puts it in the form of an imperative, in the form of a command, and fifty five times love one another. Love people, all people. Love God with your heart, mind, and soul and love your neighbor as yourself.

There are three things I want you to nail down about loving others:

Our Priority

Number one, loving others is our priority; assigned by God Himself. We read in 1 Peter 4:8, "Above all, keep loving one another earnestly, since love covers a multitude of sins." Above all, above everything else, love each other deeply. Love is the most important concept in all the Word of God. Do you understand this book is the greatest love story in the world? The Bible is the greatest love story ever written. The theme of this book is love. Love is the core value of the Christian life. Nothing is more important. Love is to be our way of life. Love is to be the way we walk, the way we talk, the way we present ourselves. Love is the path that we are to take. Love is the prescription for a happy life, a happy marriage, a happy home, happy church, and happy relationships—love is what makes it happen. So love is our assigned priority. There is nothing that trumps love, nothing greater than love. There is nothing more important than love. 1 Cor. 13:13 tell us, "and the greatest of these is . . ." What? LOVE!

Our Identity

Love is our identity. It defines us. John 13:34 says, "a new command I give you, love one another . . ." In other words, all "one anothers" as I have loved you. We are to love with God's kind of love so you must love one another. By *what*? "By your *love* all men will know that you are my disciples."

If you will love one another, people will know that you belong to God? How will people know that you are a disciple of the Lord Jesus Christ? How will people know that you love God with your heart, mind, and soul? Because you love one another! That is our badge; that is our identity.

That's how the world knows. That's what attracts the world. The world is not attracted to our church; they're not attracted to our sermons. They are attracted to the love they see in our lives. This love that is different from the world. It is a love that is much deeper and much stronger than the world. It is an unselfish love. You see, the love that He is talking about here is the word *agape*. This is God's love for us. It's totally unselfish. It means your interests are for the other person. You are not thinking about yourself, you are thinking about the other person. You are not putting yourself first; you are putting the other person first. God says when you love unselfishly, unconditionally; you don't have to jump through any hoops for Him to love you. You don't have to *do* a certain way, *act* a certain way, or *be* a certain way for Him to love you. He loves you, period. He loves you unconditionally. That's God's kind of love, and that's the love the world does not possess and cannot display. And neither can you unless you have God in your life. Unless you belong to God. Unless you have a relationship with Him. Because it is God's kind of love. "Beloved, let us love one another, for love is from God, and whoever loves has been born of God and knows God. Anyone who does not love does not know God, because God is love." *(1 John 4:7-8)*

Everyone who loves with agape love, unselfish love, is identified as one who knows God. Whoever does not love with God's kind of love, unconditional love, unselfish love does not know God. Whoever does not love with God's love does not know God, because God is love. That is His character. That is who He is. When God is being Himself, He is being love. So if God is in you, then God's love is in you. And if God's love is in you, it cannot be hidden. It will identify you as one belonging to Christ.

When I pastored in Atlanta, a man and his family started visiting our church. They were very faithful in attending and eventually joined and became very involved. David and family became very close to my family. But before I got to know him, I would speak to him at church, and every time I got around him I noticed he smelled like roses! I thought to myself, what kind of deodorant is he wearing, "Rose of Sharon?" One day my curiosity got the best of me, and I said, "David, you always smell like roses, is that your cologne? He burst out laughing and said, "Pastor, you haven't known me very long, I work at a wholesale florist. All day, every day, I am around flowers and especially roses. When I come from work, I still have the smell of roses on me!"

Every time I think of that, I remember in the Bible when Mary took that expensive perfume and anointed the feet of Jesus. Remember? John says that the odor of the perfume filled the room where they were. You get in the atmosphere of the Lord Jesus, His love, and when you leave the presence of the Lord to go out into this lost, evil world, you will have the fragrance of love about you. It identifies you with Christ.

Our Purpose

Therefore, love is our duty, our purpose. To paraphrase Mother Teresa, "we are to be like magic markers in the hand of God writing on the hearts of people." God loves you and so do I. That is our greatest assignment in this world. We are to be markers in God's hand. To write on the hearts of people, "You are loved, God loves you, and I love you!" We are to live in an atmosphere of love. We need to understand that God's love is within us and His love flows through us. We are conduits of God's love. "If anyone acknowledges that Jesus is the Son of God, God lives in them and they in God. And so we know and rely on the love God has for us. God is love. Whoever lives in love lives in God, and God in them." *(1 John 4:15-16)*

Are you catching on? We are to live lives of love. Twenty-four seven. Because God lives in us, we live lives of love on good days and on bad days, under good circumstances and under bad circumstances. As the Father loved me, so I have loved you, now remain in my love. Don't ever get outside of God's love. Don't ever stop being a conduit of God's love. Don't be a reservoir. Don't let it build up in your life; that's not God's love. God's love has to flow through you. Love is not something you work up within you. Love is something that God works out through you.

Is loving people important? It is most important. Nothing is more important. If we have nailed it down, we know that we should be a people of love, loving people, because there is nothing more important. And we should be loving people, all the time, everywhere we go, in everything that we do. The second question is then, "Who are we to love?" Jesus instructed, "love your neighbor." He said, in essence, "First love God with your heart, mind, and soul. Then, love your neighbor as yourself." Jesus explains this by giving "The Story of the Good Samaritan" (*Luke 10*). It is a fascinating story, but what is He teaching? He is answering the question, "Who is my neighbor?" Your neighbor is anyone around you who needs love. Anyone. And especially those least likely to be loved; or those least likely to be helped. It's so easy to pass by on the other side, doing our religious thing. That's what the religious men did, but then there was one man who crossed the road and went into the ditch. He loved the man and helped the man and provided for him and gave him attention and care. He got him a place to stay and paid the whole bill. That was Jesus' example of loving our neighbor. It doesn't matter who he is, it matters who is in the ditch! It matters that he needs help. He needs love. The person closest to you who needs love; love that person.

> *Love is not something you work up within you. Love is something that God works out through you.*

"If anyone says, "I love God," and hates his brother, he is a liar; for he who does not love his brother whom he has seen cannot love God whom he has not seen. And this commandment we have from him: whoever loves God must also love his brother." *(I John 4:20-21)*

So do you have a choice by loving your neighbor? No. Who is your neighbor? Anyone who is in need of love. Anyone God puts in your path that needs a kind word, or that needs help, or some encouragement.

I became a Christ-follower at the age of nine at Gulf Hills Baptist Church in Mobile, Alabama. I have wonderful memories as a young boy growing up in that small church. During my elementary school years, Mr. Busby was my Sunday School teacher. I remember he was talking to our class one time, and he said as he pointed to his watch, "Boys, here's a watch. What is it for?" We all said, "To tell the time." He said, "Well, suppose the watch doesn't keep time. What is it good for?" And we all said, "Good for nothing." He then took out a pencil and said, "What is this pencil for?" Again, we all said, "It's to write with." He then said, "Suppose the pencil won't make a mark. What is it good for?" We said, "Good for nothing." Then he took out a knife, and he said, "Boys, what is this for?" We said, "To cut things with." He said, "But suppose it won't cut anything. What is it good for?" We obediently said, "Good for nothing." Mr. Busby then looked at us in a very serious manner and said, "Boys, whatever else you do, if you do not glorify God by the way you live, and bring others to glorify God, then what are you good for?" And we all said, "Good for nothing."

Love God supremely. Love your neighbor. This is our purpose, this is why we are here. We are to live and love, reflecting the Lord Jesus Christ in such a way, that it not only brings glory to God, but it causes other people to want to glorify God. In fact, we are here for no other reason.

SECTION 3

GLORIFY

JOURNALING GUIDE

These Three is a foundational guide to understanding and practicing FAITH, HOPE, and LOVE. This section is intended as a helpful resource for spending time in God's Word. It is based on a thirty-day exercise in journaling scriptures that speak to Faith, Hope, and Love when they are manifested in a believer's life.

The "3 for 30" journaling guide is straightforward, including suggested observations and prayers. After the thirty days have concluded, I encourage you to continue in daily W.O.R.D. Journaling.

W.O.R.D. JOURNALING

First of all, DON'T RUSH as you go through these steps. It will take time to do your devotion time this way, but you will eventually begin to take His Word, study it for yourself, discover His truths, and hear His voice speaking to you personally through the scripture.

W stands for WORD OF GOD. This is where the scripture passage that you are reading is listed.

O stands for OBSERVATION. This is where you dig a little deeper to figure out what the passage is saying. Read the passage and simplify each verse down to its main idea. Think of this step as summarizing the verse. To help, ask yourself: Who's speaking? What's the main subject? Where is this taking place? When did it happen?

R stands for REFLECTION. This is where you take it one step further to determine what it means for us as individuals. For each of the simplified verses from the *Observation* section, write out a spiritual truth. If you get stuck, ask yourself: What are the characters doing or not doing that we should or shouldn't be doing? Is there a command we need to obey? Is there a promise that God makes? Is there a warning we need to remember? Is there an example we need to follow?

D stands for DISCUSS. This is your opportunity to be honest with God. Ask God to help you live out the truth you have discovered. Write out your prayer. In addition, ask God to give you an opportunity to share what you have learned with someone else that day. Share your journey through the WORD!

The following *3 for 30* will serve as an example and guide to help you get started. As you go through your own W.O.R.D. Journaling, here are three key ideas to remember:

- *Do not take on too many verses!* It is more important for you to understand one to five verses than to finish twenty and have no idea what they mean.

- *Do take your time!* This process is designed to place you in God's Word and focus your attention on it. Give yourself plenty of time (about 20 minutes) for the Lord to speak to you.

- *Do not ignore the instruction you receive!* James 1:22 says, "But don't just listen to God's Word. You must do what it says . . ." (*NIV*) Apply these teachings to your daily life.

3 FOR 30

According to your Faith

Word of God

"When he entered the house, the blind men came to him, and Jesus said to them, 'Do you believe that I am able to do this?' They said to him, 'Yes, Lord.' Then he touched their eyes, saying, 'According to your faith be it done to you.' And their eyes were opened." *Matthew 9:28-30a*

Observation

~What does it say?~

God responds to faith. God blesses people who have faith. Jesus asked if they believed He was able to open their eyes. Their answer was positive, and faith-filled. It was also a humble, submissive answer, "Lord." It secured Jesus' healing touch. As He touched them, He said that His power had flowed "according (in response) to (their) faith."

_____

_____

_____

_____

Reflection

~What does it mean? What do I do?~

Faith touches the heart of God and moves the hand of God. Crying, complaining, and self-pity do not motivate God to act. Faith does. Our prayers are not powerful because they are long and elaborate. Rather, they are powerful only when we offer them to God in faith believing He will act.

_____

_____

_____

_____

_____

_____

Discuss

Take a few minutes and talk to the Lord. Ask Him to help you live out your 'truth' today. Make it an honest and personal discussion. For example, "Lord Jesus, I am praying the prayer of the blind men today…"Yes, Lord." I believe you are able to do this (name what you are trusting God for today). I am not hoping you will act, I know you can and will because it is your will to do so." Finally, ask the Lord for an opportunity to discuss with someone what you have learned today.

3 FOR 30

Abounding in Hope

Word of God:

"May the God of hope fill you with all joy and peace in believing, so that by the power of the Holy Spirit you may abound in hope." (*Romans 15:13*)

Observation

~What does it say?~

God is able to work miracles and offer us hope regardless of how bad things may seem. And He adds "joy and peace" to hope. "All" means that He gives "mega-joy" and "super-peace." The Holy Spirit is an artesian well that produces this hope.

_____

_____

_____

_____

_____

_____

Reflection

~What does it mean? What do I do?~

We cannot produce hope; we can only display it. It comes when we abide in Christ, and allow God's Spirit to fill us from within. He changes our dismay into assurance, celebration, and tranquility of the soul. Sadness and worry depart. Joy and peace arrive.

_____

_____

_____

_____

_____

_____

Discuss

Take a few minutes and talk to the Lord. Ask Him to help you live out your 'truth' today. Make it an honest and personal discussion. For example, *"Lord Jesus, I know there is hope for my future. True hope comes from you, not from mere positive attitudes or wishful thinking. As I abide in you, Jesus, may your Spirit fill me with hope from within."* Finally, ask the Lord for an opportunity to discuss with someone what you have learned today.

3 FOR 30

The Love of God

Word of God:

"For God so loved the world, that he gave his only Son, that whoever believes in him should not perish but have eternal life." (*John 3:16*)

Observation

~What does it say?~

God's love is intense. He loves us more than anything else He has created. His love is universal, He loves everyone. And He demonstrated His love when Jesus died for our sins. He did not just *say* He loved us; He *showed us* He loved us!

_____

_____

_____

_____

_____

_____

Reflection
~What does it mean? What do I do?~

Imagine how much God loves you. Nothing you can do will cause Him to love you more, or less. He has chosen to love you by His grace. But God's love is demanding: "That *whoever* believes in Him." No one can be neutral about Jesus. A person must trust Him for salvation, or reject Him. The reward for trusting Jesus is abundant, everlasting life. By faith, accept and enjoy His great love today.

_____
_____
_____
_____
_____
_____

Discuss

Take a few minutes and talk to the Lord. Ask Him to help you live out your 'truth' today. Make it an honest and personal discussion. For example *"God thank you for loving me, before I ever thought of loving you. Thank you that your love for me is not determined by my actions or attitude. There is nothing I can do so great as to cause you to love my any more than you already do. Help me to enjoy your great love today as I trust you."* Finally, ask the Lord for an opportunity to discuss with someone what you have learned today.

3 FOR 30

Filled with the Spirit

Word of God:

"And do not get drunk with wine, for that is debauchery, but be filled with the Spirit." (*Ephesians 5:18*)

Observation

~What does it say?~

A person who gets "drunk with wine" walks, talks, thinks, and acts differently than when he is sober. Likewise a Christian who is "filled (intoxicated) with the Spirit walks, talks, thinks, and acts differently than a self-centered, worldly, carnal person. At the point of conversion, the Spirit baptizes us into Christ. After that, we can be filled with the Spirit many times. So, there is one baptism of the Spirit but many fillings.

_____

_____

_____

_____

_____

_____

Reflection

~What does it mean? What do I do?~

We are filled with the Spirit the same way we are saved —by grace, through faith. We simply confess all known sin, and then ask the Lord to fill us (Luke 11:13). To be filled with the Spirit is not to receive more of Him, it is to release His power that is already within us. He is a mighty indwelling river of living water, and He wants out!

_____

_____

_____

_____

_____

_____

Discuss

Take a few minutes and talk to the Lord. Ask Him to help you live out your 'truth' today. Make it an honest and personal discussion. For example, *"Heavenly Father, I know that you want me to walk in your power. You have not left me to fight for myself alone. Through the power of your indwelling Spirit, you have given me everything I need to live as more than a conqueror. Release your Mighty River in me today! Amen."* Finally, ask the Lord for an opportunity to discuss with someone what you have learned today.

3 FOR 30

The Purpose of Trials

Word of God:

"Count it all joy, my brothers, when you meet trials of various kinds, for you know that the testing of your faith produces steadfastness. And let steadfastness have its full effect, that you may be perfect and complete, lacking in nothing." (*James 1:2-4*)

Observation

~*What does it say?*~

Becoming a Christian does not exempt us from facing difficulties. We will have troubles in this world. We can have joy like the early apostles did when they suffered. When a believer is tested, it gives him the opportunity to respond maturely in faith and obedience.

_____
_____
_____
_____
_____
_____

Reflection

~What does it mean? What do I do?~

We are to greet trials with joy. Times of testing produce "steadfastness." The word "perfect" refers to maturity. In other words, trials help us grow in grace and in Christlikeness. Whenever we are squeezed by trouble, the joy of Jesus should come out. Unbelievers will see and take notice.

_____

_____

_____

_____

_____

_____

Discuss

Take a few minutes and talk to the Lord. Ask Him to help you live out your 'truth' today. Make it an honest and personal discussion. For example, *"Lord Jesus, I recognize that I WILL face trial and tribulation. Yet, you are able to make me victorious. Help me to count every difficulty as a glorious stepping stone that will lead to joy, endurance, and maturity. I know you have a purpose in my trials."* Finally, ask the Lord for an opportunity to discuss with someone what you have learned today.

3 FOR 30

Loving Sinners

Word of God:

"Jesus stood up and said to her, 'Woman, where are they? Has no one condemned you?' She said, 'No one, Lord.' And Jesus said, 'Neither do I condemn you; go, and from now on sin no more.'" (*John 8:10-11*)

Observation

~What does it say?~

To the woman caught in adultery, Jesus responded in love. He loved the sinner while He hated the sin. In His words, He lifted up *both* the sinner and the standard of God's Word. Jesus rebuked the response of the Pharisees which valued religion and not God's mercy.

_____

_____

_____

_____

_____

_____

_____

_____

_____

Reflection
~What does it mean? What do I do?~

This is how Jesus treats us when we sin, and it is how we ought to treat other sinners also. If a bridge is out, we must first care for the victims who have fallen into the gorge. But we must also warn others not to run off the bridge. That balance is the response of love, and that is how we must respond to sinners.

_____

_____

_____

_____

_____

_____

Discuss

Take a few minutes and talk to the Lord. Ask Him to help you live out your 'truth' today. Make it an honest and personal discussion. For example, *"Lord Jesus, thank you for loving me in my sin. May I follow your example, and love and lift up fallen sinners. And may I also encourage and warn them not to fall again."* Finally, ask the Lord for an opportunity to discuss with someone what you have learned today.

3 FOR 30

Grace Set Free

Word of God:

"That is why it depends on faith, in order that the promise may rest on grace and be guaranteed to all his offspring – not only to the adherent to the law but also to the one who shares the faith of Abraham." (*Romans 14:16*)

Observation

~What does it say?~

Simply, without faith, you'll never know grace, the unmerited love and favor of God. The only way to get it, to set it free in your life, is by faith. On the other hand, unbelief holds grace prisoner. We have a written 'guarantee': Faith relies on God's promises, not our own wish list. We are to rely on what God has said, rooted in His Word and His promises.

Reflection

~What does it mean? What do I do?~

God is full of grace, Amazing Grace, overflowing to me. But the only way I can get it—to set it free—is by faith. And in order to increase my faith, I need to hear God's Word (see Romans 10:7). What can I do today in light of this truth?

_____

_____

_____

_____

_____

_____

Discuss

Take a few minutes and talk to the Lord. Ask Him to help you live out your 'truth' today. Make it an honest and personal discussion. For example, *"Lord Jesus, help my unbelief. Help me to hold fast to your promises and therefore set your grace free in my life. Please give me a greater desire to study Your Word daily, and to share those truths with those around me."* Finally, ask the Lord for an opportunity to discuss what you have learned today.

3 FOR 30

Those Without Hope

Word **of God:**

"But we do not want you to be uninformed, brothers, about those who are asleep, that you may not grieve as others do who have no hope." (*I Thessalonians 4:13*)

Observation

~What does it say?~

The unbeliever is exposed in times of death. Their normal confident smiles are replaced by expressions of shock, confusion, and grief. They are tricked by Satan in living for the moment, acting fearless and unconcerned about tomorrow. They are those "who have no hope."

_____

_____

_____

_____

_____

_____

_____

_____

_____

Reflection

~What does it mean? What do I do?~

How differently the Christian grieves! In the hearts of the redeemed, there is the reality that the deceased loved one is in a better place. They are absent from the body and present with the Lord (II Cor. 5:8). An overarching, triumphant promise sustains the heart: I am the resurrection and the life. Whoever believes in me, though he die, yet shall he live" (John 11:25).

_____

_____

_____

_____

_____

_____

Discuss

Take a few minutes and talk to the Lord. Ask Him to help you live out your 'truth' today. Make it an honest and personal discussion. For example, *"Lord Jesus, I am determined to share the Gospel to anyone and everyone you bring into my life. Apart from Jesus, they have no hope of life after death, only eternal separation from you."* Finally, ask the Lord for an opportunity to discuss with someone what you have learned today.

3 FOR 30

The Love of God

Word of God:

"the LORD appeared to him from far away. I have loved you with an everlasting love; therefore I have continued my faithfulness to you." *(Jeremiah 31:3)*

Observation

~What does it say?~

"I have loved you." Before we chose to love God, He loved us first. He initiated the love relationship we enjoy with Him . . . "with an everlasting love." There has never been a time that God did not love you. "I have continued my faithfulness to you." Though we deserve eternal punishment, God deals with us with kindness and compassion.

_____

_____

_____

_____

_____

_____

_____

_____

_____

Reflection
~What does it mean? What do I do?~

God's love is amazing! He does not force anyone to love Him, because true love cannot be coerced. God initiates the love relationship, and we are to respond willingly. God loved you first. He will always love you. He loves you faithfully.

_____

_____

_____

_____

_____

_____

Discuss
Take a few minutes and talk to the Lord. Ask Him to help you live out your 'truth' today. Make it an honest and personal discussion. For example, *"Loving Heavenly Father, before the foundations of world, you loved me. Thank you for loving me in spite of my sin and selfishness. Regardless of what I do, or what happens in my life, I know you will love me forever. As I wonder how much you love me, I consider the Cross, and the sacrifice of your only Son . . . for me! Amen."* Finally, ask the Lord for an opportunity to discuss with someone what you have learned today.

3 FOR 30

Fire in my Bones

Word of God:

"If I say, 'I will not mention him, or speak any more in his name,' there is in my heart as it were a burning fire shut up in my bones, and I am weary with holding it in, and I cannot." (*Jeremiah 20:9*)

Observation

~What does it say?~

Jeremiah was a prophet during a very difficult time in Judah's history. During this time, he would faithfully deliver God's messages, but the people would not heed God's warnings. In fact, they increased in wickedness. Jeremiah became weary and considered quitting his ministry. At that critical moment, God's Word became a burning fire within his heart that had to be released. He HAD to preach!

_____
_____
_____
_____
_____
_____

Reflection

~What does it mean? What do I do?~

Does the Gospel of Jesus Christ burn within you? As Christians, we should find it difficult to hold back the fiery message of Jesus Christ. This world needs to hear from those who will share passionately about Jesus with God's fire in their bones!

_____

_____

_____

_____

_____

_____

Discuss

Take a few minutes and talk to the Lord. Ask Him to help you live out your 'truth' today. Make it an honest and personal discussion. For example, *"Lord, ignite a fresh flame of evangelistic zeal within my heart today. May your Word be like a fire within my bones! Like a grandparent who loves to talk about their grandchildren, may I speak of my Jesus."* Finally, ask the Lord for an opportunity to discuss with someone what you have learned today.

3 FOR 30

The Lord who Sanctifies

Word of God:

"Keep my statutes and do them; I am the Lord who sanctifies you." *(Leviticus 20:8)*

Observation

~What does it say?~

In our text God reminded Israel that He was the One who had sanctified and set them apart from all the other nations as His. They belonged to Him, and they were to imitate Him in His holiness.

_____
_____
_____
_____
_____
_____
_____
_____
_____

Reflection

~What does it mean? What do I do?~

We as Christians are set apart and sanctified by God. He has called us out from a life of darkness and sin to a holy life of light and obedience. We are to walk, talk, think, and act differently than the people of this world. God is still Jehovah-Mekadesh, "The Lord who sanctifies." He is holy, and He has sanctified us to be holy.

_____

_____

_____

_____

_____

_____

Discuss

Take a few minutes and talk to the Lord. Ask Him to help you live out your 'truth' today. Make it an honest and personal discussion. For example, *"Heavenly Father, thank you for setting me apart to be one of your chosen vessels. May I bear your name while living in this unholy world. Fill me with your power and purity. Make me delightfully different and pleasantly peculiar."* Finally, ask the Lord for an opportunity to discuss with someone what you have learned today.

THESE THREE

3 FOR 30

Together in Unity

Word of God:
"Behold, how good and pleasant it is when brothers dwell together in unity." *(Psalm 133:1)*

Observation
~What does it say?~

The psalmist said that it is "good and pleasant" for God's people to live in harmony with one another. Everyone who is born again is a child of God whether they agree with us on every matter or not. When we argue with one another, it grieves the heart of God and also damages our witness with the lost world.

_____
_____
_____
_____
_____
_____
_____
_____
_____

Reflection
~What does it mean? What do I do?~

We must seek to build bridges in Christ's body, not walls. A fighting, fussing church and a divisive Christian are both tools in Satan's hand. The world will know that we are Jesus' followers only when we love one another.

_____

_____

_____

_____

_____

_____

Discuss

Take a few minutes and talk to the Lord. Ask Him to help you live out your 'truth' today. Make it an honest and personal discussion. For example, *"Heavenly Father, help me to 'preserve the unity of the Spirit in the bond of peace' (Ephesians 4:3). Give me a love for all Christians, even with those to whom I differ. May I not emphasize the differences, but focus on what we have in common... the same Savior and the same Lord."* Finally, ask the Lord for an opportunity to discuss with someone what you have learned today.

3 FOR 30

Moving Mountains

Word of God:

"Truly, I say to you, whoever says to this mountain, 'Be taken up and thrown into the sea,' and does not doubt in his heart, but believes that what he says will come to pass, it will be done for him." *(Mark 11:22-23)*

Observation

~What does it say?~

As Jesus entered Jerusalem one day, He saw a fruitless fig tree and cursed it. The next day when He and His disciples passed by, they marveled that it had completely withered. Jesus used the occasion to teach them how to move any problem, or "mountain" they would face. To see a mountain moved, they needed to trust in God and speak to that mountain in faith. Faith moves the hand of God.

_____

_____

_____

_____

_____

_____

_____

_____

_____

Reflection

~What does it mean? What do I do?~

God is able to move any mountain you face today. If you have the faith, He has the power. Stop focusing on the mountain, and start focusing on Jesus. God still works wonders for those who believe in His power, stand on His Word, and speak in faith to the obstacles they confront.

_____

_____

_____

_____

_____

_____

Discuss

Take a few minutes and talk to the Lord. Ask Him to help you live out your 'truth' today. Make it an honest and personal discussion. For example, *"God, you are good, omnipotent, and gracious. Give me a promise from your Word to build my faith. I will speak that word to my mountain. I will tell it to be uprooted and move in Jesus' name!"* Finally, ask the Lord for an opportunity to discuss with someone what you have learned today.

3 FOR 30

Loving the Lord

Word of God:

"And he answered, 'You shall love the Lord your God with all your heart and with all your soul and with all your strength and with all your mind, and your neighbor as yourself.'" *(Luke 10:27)*

Observation

~What does it say?~

Loving God means seeing God in all things; thinking of Him at all times; keeping your mind continually fixed upon God; acknowledging Him in all your ways. It means beginning, continuing, and ending all your thoughts, words and works, to the glory of His name. This is the person who loves God with all of his heart, his might, and strength, and his intellect.

_____
_____
_____
_____
_____
_____
_____
_____
_____

Reflection

~What does it mean? What do I do?~

We should love the Lord our God more than anything else. Nothing is to take precedence over Him, not our desires, our will, or anything else. God is always first. We are to love God with all of our soul. We are to be ready to give up our lives to honor God, if it is required. We are to endure all types of ridicule and torment for His sake. That is part of loving God.

_____

_____

_____

_____

_____

_____

Discuss

Take a few minutes and talk to the Lord. Ask Him to help you live out your 'truth' today. Make it an honest and personal discussion. For example, *"Lord, help me to better love you, and help me to love others and see them how you see them."* Finally, ask the Lord for an opportunity to discuss with someone what you have learned today.

3 FOR 30

Doing a Great Work

Word of God:

"And I sent messengers to them, saying, "I am doing a great work and I cannot come down. Why should the work stop while I leave it and come down to you?" *(Nehemiah 6:3)*

Observation

~What does it say?~

Nehemiah had an important work to accomplish. God had called him to return to Jerusalem from exile to re-build the great wall that had been destroyed by the Babylonians. Nehemiah faced severe opposition from the Gentile neighbors. Nevertheless, he refused to be distracted. Though they tried to lure him into a meeting so they could kill him, Nehemiah refused to leave the work.

_____

_____

_____

_____

_____

_____

_____

_____

Reflection

~What does it mean? What do I do?~

Because of obedience, focus, and passion, the wall was completed in only 52 days! If you are saved, God has a great work for you. It may seem insignificant to others, but that does not matter. You must discover God's will for you and then go for it! Remember, God's work is a great work! You must not come down until it is finished.

_____

_____

_____

_____

_____

_____

Discuss

Take a few minutes and talk to the Lord. Ask Him to help you live out your 'truth' today. Make it an honest and personal discussion. For example, *"God, what is the work you have for me? What is the task you have for me to accomplish? As you reveal your will for me, I will not be distracted. I will focus on You and will not allow the enemy to draw me away."* Finally, ask the Lord for an opportunity to discuss with someone what you have learned today.

3 FOR 30

Anything that is Worthless

Word of God:

"I will walk with integrity of heart within my house; I will not set before my eyes anything that is worthless. I hate the work of those who fall away; it shall not cling to me." *(Psalm 101:2b-3)*

Observation

~What does it say?~

The Psalmist wanted to live a godly life in his home. He wanted to live as a man of "integrity" before God and his family members. He determined not to set "anything worthless" before his eyes in his home. He was referring to an idol. He said that such a thing would "cling" to him. He wanted to be morally and spiritually pure, so he declared war on any vile or vulgar thing within his home.

_____

_____

_____

_____

_____

_____

Reflection

~What does it mean? What do I do?~

Christianity should begin at home. Our homes should be havens of the Holy Spirit where Christ is honored, worshipped, and obeyed. Nothing in our home should dishonor the name of Jesus Christ. Everything that comes across our televisions, computers, and smart devices should be monitored to see if it pleases Him. If there is the slightest question of suitability, we must remove it. It is better to err on the side of caution than to invite tragedy.

_____

_____

_____

_____

_____

_____

Discuss

Ask the Lord to help you live out your 'truth' today. Make it an honest and personal discussion. For example *"Lord Jesus, is there anything in my home that could hinder my walk with you? I do not want to give Satan a foothold to wreak havoc in my family. I surrender every part of my home to you; I reject anything that is 'worthless.'"* Finally, ask the Lord for an opportunity to discuss with someone what you have learned today.

3 FOR 30

Love One Another

Word of God:

"A new commandment I give to you, that you love one another: just as I have loved you, you also are to love one another. By this all people will know that you are my disciples, if you have love for one another." *(John 13:34-35)*

Observation

~What does it say?~

When Jesus was asked about the greatest of God's commandments, He answered that it was to love God (Mark 12:30). The second greatest commandment is to love other people (Mark 12:31). The text teaches that our love for fellow believers is the primary indication that we are truly Christ's disciples. We are most like Jesus when we love one another.

_____

_____

_____

_____

_____

_____

Reflection

~What does it mean? What do I do?~

Christian love is the greatest testimony of the change Jesus brings to a person's life. When unbelievers see true love among believers, it causes them to desire to know more about Christ. Genuine, compassionate, and caring love is so seldom seen, that it catches the non-Christian off guard when they see it. Love is the bridge that must be built to carry the Gospel to our lost world.

_____

_____

_____

_____

_____

_____

Discuss

Take a few minutes and talk to the Lord. Ask Him to help you live out your 'truth' today. Make it an honest and personal discussion. For example, *"Lord Jesus, I want others to see my love for you and other people, especially other believers. Fill me with your love for others today."* Finally, ask the Lord for an opportunity to discuss with someone what you have learned today.

3 FOR 30

The Unseen Lord

Word of God:

"Though you have not seen him, you love him. Though you do not now see him, you believe in him and rejoice with joy that is inexpressible and filled with glory." *(1 Peter 1:8)*

Observation

~What does it say?~

We serve a God we have never seen. Jesus, God's Son, was obviously seen while He was on this earth, but no one has ever beheld God the Father. In our text, Peter addressed people who came to faith after Christ had ascended back to heaven. Like them, though we have never seen Jesus, we know Him!

_____

_____

_____

_____

_____

_____

_____

_____

Reflection
~What does it mean? What do I do?~

Christians do not see and believe. Rather, we believe without seeing. We walk by faith, not by sight (2 Cor. 5:7). Though we have not seen Him, we trust Jesus now and forever. The source of our joy is not of this world. The fountain of our joy is Christ.

_____

_____

_____

_____

_____

_____

Discuss

Take a few minutes and talk to the Lord. Ask Him to help you live out your 'truth' today. Make it an honest and personal discussion. For example, *"Lord Jesus, the joy you offer surpasses anything this world has to offer. One day I will see you, the One who saved me by your grace. Until then, help me to love, trust, and rejoice in my unseen God."* Finally, ask the Lord for an opportunity to discuss with someone what you have learned today.

3 FOR 30

The Second Coming

Word of God:

"Men of Galilee, why do you stand looking into heaven? This Jesus, who was taken up from you into heaven, will come in the same way as you saw him go into heaven." *(Acts 1:11)*

Observation

~What does it say?~

In our text, the angels promised that Jesus would one day come back to this earth just as he had left it. He ascended to heaven in the clouds with great glory. He will return the same way, being escorted by angels and God's saints. Jesus left this earth, but He will come again!

_____

_____

_____

_____

_____

_____

_____

_____

Reflection

~What does it mean? What do I do?~

Christ's return was predicted in the Old Testament and in the New Testament. Like His first coming, Christ's return will be an actual, precise event. Jesus will return literally, bodily, and visibly at His Second Coming! His glory will be revealed, His heavenly army will be deployed, and His enemies will be defeated . . . Jesus will reign as Judge and King!

_____

_____

_____

_____

_____

_____

Discuss

Take a few minutes and talk to the Lord. Ask Him to help you live out your 'truth' today. Make it an honest and personal discussion. For example, *"Lord Jesus, I know this world will grow spiritually darker as the end of time draws near. Help me to shine brighter and brighter with each passing day. I long for your rule and reign on this earth."* Finally, ask the Lord for an opportunity to discuss with someone what you have learned today.

3 FOR 30

Making Praise a Priority

Word of God:

"I will bless the LORD at all times; His praise shall continually be in my mouth." (*Psalm 34:1*)

Observation

~What does it say?~

King David made praising God a priority. "I will bless the LORD.' Praise is a choice. David praised God regardless of the circumstances. David praised God everyday, "at all times." David also knew that praise in the heart demands expression on the lips. "His praise shall continually be in my mouth." True love always results in verbal expression.

_____
_____
_____
_____
_____
_____
_____
_____
_____

Reflection

~What does it mean? What do I do?~

To please God, we too must prioritize perpetual praise. On the mountaintop or in the valley, we should worship our Lord. Our Father wants to hear His children praising Him. Praise is a choice that must become a lifestyle. It demands verbal expression. The redeemed of the Lord must say so!

_____

_____

_____

_____

_____

_____

Discuss

Take a few minutes and talk to the Lord. Ask Him to help you live out your 'truth' today. Make it an honest and personal discussion. For example, *"Living Lord, I open my heart and mouth in worship and praise to you. I choose this day to worship you. Help me to keep a song of praise ever on my lips. If I am breathing, I want to be praising you. Amen."* Finally, ask the Lord for an opportunity to discuss with someone what you have learned today.

3 FOR 30

A Call to Holiness

Word of God:

"You shall be holy to me, for I the Lord am holy and have separated you from the peoples, that you should be mine." *(Leviticus 20:26)*

Observation

~What does it say?~

God is holy. He is perfectly pure. God can never think, do, or say anything remotely sinful. God also desires for His children to be holy. When He grants us salvation, he sanctifies us and sets us apart from other people to be His.

_____

_____

_____

_____

_____

_____

_____

_____

_____

Reflection

~What does it mean? What do I do?~

As a child of God, you have been saved to belong distinctly to God. He has called you out of this world to be an instrument of honor for His glory. You are to be in it, but not of it. The world culture today that is anti-Jesus, anti-church, and anti-Bible must not determine the way you act, think, or speak. Jesus is holy and He expects holiness from you.

_____

_____

_____

_____

_____

_____

Discuss

Take a few minutes and talk to the Lord. Ask Him to help you live out your 'truth' today. Make it an honest and personal discussion. For example, *"Holy Father, create a clean heart within me. Make me a vessel of honor for your glory. Help me to be different from the world. Cause me to love you more and to despise the things of this world that are not of the Father. Amen."* Finally, ask the Lord for an opportunity to discuss with someone what you have learned today.

3 FOR 30

True Love

Word of God:

"Many waters cannot quench love, neither can floods drown it. If a man offered for love all the wealth of his house, he would be utterly despised." *(Song of Solomon 8:7)*

Observation

~What does it say?~

Our text says two things about true love. First, it is indestructible. Despite the difficulties a married couple could encounter, love can see them through. Second, true love cannot be sold. True love cannot be prostituted. Rather, the lovers must give it to one another mutually and freely.

_____

_____

_____

_____

_____

_____

_____

_____

Reflection

~What does it mean? What do I do?~

Solomon wrote this book as a love song to his young bride. The blessing of romantic love that leads to a life-long marriage is a gift from God. It weathers life's fiercest storms. It is more priceless than silver or gold. If God has blessed you with that gift, guard it and cherish it. It is the most precious treasure you possess.

_____

_____

_____

_____

_____

_____

Discuss

Take a few minutes and talk to the Lord. Ask Him to help you live out your 'truth' today. Make it an honest and personal discussion. For example, *"Heavenly Father, in your Word it says that love '...bears all things, believes all things, hopes all things, endures all things. Love never fails'(1 Corinthians 13:7-8a). Help me to live out this truth in my marriage. This love you have given me cannot be purchased with money; it is a gift from you. May I cherish it as such."* Finally, ask the Lord for an opportunity to discuss with someone what you have learned today.

3 FOR 30

The God of Creation

Word of God:

"In the beginning, God created the heavens and the earth." *(Genesis 1:1)*

Observation

~What does it say?~

When time as we know it began, God alone existed. He existed immutably as the infinite uncaused Cause. All-powerful, all-knowing, and eternal, He created everything from atoms to solar systems through the power of His spoken Word. He was and is the source of life. Only God can create life out of nothing. That is the power of our creating God!

_____
_____
_____
_____
_____
_____
_____
_____
_____

Reflection
~What does it mean? What do I do?~

The fact of creation demands a Creator. There is a God, and we can know Him personally! We are not an accidental, random mutation that evolved over billions of years. God created us in His image, for His glory. He will recreate us through salvation in Jesus Christ. All praise and glory to our God of creation!

_____

_____

_____

_____

_____

_____

Discuss

Take a few minutes and talk to the Lord. Ask Him to help you live out your 'truth' today. Make it an honest and personal discussion. For example, *"God of Creation and Redemption, you are the all-powerful God. Man may create using pre-existing building blocks, but only You can create life out of absolutely nothing. Thank you for creating me in your image, for your glory. May my life and actions give you praise."* Finally, ask the Lord for an opportunity to discuss with someone what you have learned today.

3 FOR 30

Hope in His Return

Word of God:

"He who testifies to these things says, 'Surely I am coming soon.' Amen. Come, Lord Jesus!" *(Revelation 22:20)*

Observation

~What does it say?~

Jesus is coming back. Though only Christians will see Jesus at the Rapture, everyone on earth will see Him at His return. Those who rejected Him as Savior will mourn because He is coming to judge them, not to save them. On that day every knee will bow before Jesus. Though evil men curse His name today, they will bless His name on that day.

Reflection

~What does it mean? What do I do?~

Jesus' return is the apex of all the end-time events described in Revelation. Jesus will ultimately touch down on the Mount of Olives, and will rule the earth from Jerusalem for a thousand years. The final judgment will then occur, followed by the destruction of the earth and heavens. A new heaven and earth, along with the New Jerusalem will appear. There the saints will live forever. Are you ready for the end of time?

_____

_____

_____

_____

_____

_____

Discuss

Take a few minutes and talk to the Lord. Ask Him to help you live out your 'truth' today. Make it an honest and personal discussion. For example, *"King Jesus, you inaugurated history, and will consummate it as well. You promised to come quickly. Amen. Come Lord Jesus!"* Finally, ask the Lord for an opportunity to discuss with someone what you have learned today.

3 FOR 30

Our Father

Word of God:

"Pray then like this: 'Our Father in heaven, hallowed be your name.'" *(Matthew 6:9a)*

Observation

~What does it say?~

In the Model Prayer, Jesus instructed His disciples to address God as "Father," because they were His beloved children. That concept was never taught in the Old Testament. To most Jews in Jesus' day, it would seem blasphemous to refer to God as one's "Father."

Reflection

~What does it mean? What do I do?~

God is not distant and impersonal. Those who have received Christ as Savior have indeed become children of God (John 1:12). Paul encouraged the early Christians to cry out to God by calling Him their "Abba" which means "Father" because His indwelling Spirit had made them children of God (Romans 8:15). You are God's precious child, and He loves you dearly.

_____

_____

_____

_____

_____

_____

Discuss

Take a few minutes and talk to the Lord. Ask Him to help you live out your 'truth' today. Make it an honest and personal discussion. For example, *"Dear God, thank you for being my Heavenly Father. You are my 'Abba' . . . my 'Father.' I will seek to draw near to you as a child to their father. I will cry out to you in times of joy as well as points of anguish and desperation. I am your precious child. Amen."* Finally, ask the Lord for an opportunity to discuss with someone what you have learned today.

3 FOR 30

God Clears the Way

Word of **God**:

"Trust in the Lord with all your heart, and do not lean on your own understanding. In all your ways acknowledge him, and he will make straight your paths." *(Proverbs 3:5-6)*

Observation

~What does it say?~

God is saying that He will clear a path for us by removing any obstruction in our way. He says to us, "Just put your hand in Mine and I will take you where you need to go."

_____

_____

_____

_____

_____

_____

_____

_____

Reflection

~What does it mean? What do I do?~

God is bigger than your problem. God knows how to clear the way for His children. He will make a way for you though there seems to be no way. You must trust Him and walk by faith.

_____

_____

_____

_____

_____

_____

Discuss

Take a few minutes and talk to the Lord. Ask Him to help you live out your 'truth' today. Make it an honest and personal discussion. For example, *"God, you are bigger than my problem. You can level any mountain, fill in any valley, straighten any crooked path, and smooth out any rough road. Help me to trust you and walk by faith."* Finally, ask the Lord for an opportunity to discuss with someone what you have learned today.

3 FOR 30

Grow in Grace

Word of God:

"But grow in the grace and knowledge of our Lord and Savior Jesus Christ. To him be the glory both now and to the day of eternity. Amen." *(2 Peter 3:18)*

Observation

~What does it say?~

Peter is referring to the process of God's children maturing spiritually. When a person becomes a Christian, he is born again and becomes a spiritual baby who needs to grow and develop (I Peter 2:2). Our text says that as a Christian matures, at least two things will happen. First, he will "grow in the grace." Second, he will "grow in the knowledge."

Reflection

~What does it mean? What do I do?~

To grow in grace is to become more merciful toward others. You will extend forgiveness, restoration, and compassion to others. To grow in knowledge is to not only know about Jesus, but will literally know Him. Your increased intimacy with Christ will manifest itself in both in passionate worship and obedient service.

_____

_____

_____

_____

_____

_____

Discuss

Take a few minutes and talk to the Lord. Ask Him to help you live out your 'truth' today. Make it an honest and personal discussion. For example, *"Lord Jesus, I want to grow in grace and knowledge. I want to grow spiritually. Develop in me maturity as I read and study the Bible; and as I pray and worship. Help me to grow in grace as I build community with other believers and witness to unbelievers. Amen."* Finally, ask the Lord for an opportunity to discuss with someone what you have learned today.

3 FOR 30

Great is your Faithfulness

Word of God:

"The steadfast love of the Lord never ceases: his mercies never come to an end; they are new every morning; great is your faithfulness." *(Lamentations 3:22-23)*

Observation

~What does it say?~

The prophet Jeremiah lived during a dismal period in Judah's history. God's people had persistently engaged in idolatry and other sins, and when judgment finally came, it was worse than could have been imagined. Yet God promised Jeremiah that there was hope for Judah's future. The Lord would allow a remnant to return and rebuild Jerusalem. Jeremiah praised the Lord for His magnificent faithfulness that displayed such love and mercy on the rebellious nation.

_____

_____

_____

_____

_____

_____

Reflection
~What does it mean? What do I do?~

God is faithful to us as well. Though we are sinners by nature and choice, He consistently supplies a fresh batch of love and compassion for us each morning. Though we have not been faithful to Him, He remains ever faithful to us. He allows us to begin again.

_____

_____

_____

_____

_____

_____

Discuss

Take a few minutes and talk to the Lord. Ask Him to help you live out your 'truth' today. Make it an honest and personal discussion. For example, *"Heavenly Father, I praise you today for your mercy! Yesterday is gone. Today is a new start. O Lord, great is Your faithfulness!"* Finally, ask the Lord for an opportunity to discuss with someone what you have learned today.

3 FOR 30

Authority over the Enemy

Word of God:

"Behold, I have given you authority to tread on serpents and scorpions, and over all the power of the enemy, and nothing shall hurt you." *(Luke 10:19)*

Observation

~What does it say?~

Jesus told the early disciples that He had given them authority over demonic "serpents and scorpions" they faced as they preached the Gospel and healed the sick. They had authority "over all the power of the enemy." No demon could harm them as long as they were walking obediently with Him.

_____

_____

_____

_____

_____

_____

_____

_____

_____

Reflection

~What does it mean? What do I do?~

Christians have been deputized with authority over demonic spirits. The New Testament describes many instances when Jesus' disciples took authority over demons, bound them, and cast them out of people. That same power is still available to every believer today by faith and obedience. As a soldier of the cross you are to engage in spiritual warfare.

_____

_____

_____

_____

_____

_____

Discuss

Take a few minutes and talk to the Lord. Ask Him to help you live out your 'truth' today. Make it an honest and personal discussion. For example, *"Lord Jesus, I believe the devil is real, and he may be attacking me or someone I love right now. He is a roaring lion, seeking someone to devour. As a Christian, I am to man my battle stations! I submit myself completely to you, and I will stand up, resist the devil and watch him flee! Amen."* Finally, ask the Lord for an opportunity to discuss with someone what you have learned today.

3 FOR 30

First Love

Word of God:

"But I have this against you, that you have abandoned the love you had at first." *(Revelation 2:4)*

Observation

~What does it say?~

The Church at Ephesus was a remarkable church with an outstanding history. Yet, Jesus found a fatal flaw in that fellowship. They had left their first love for Him. The thrill and passion they once had for Jesus had waned into a mechanical, ritualistic habit of "going through the motions." The honeymoon was over, and the Groom was upset!

_____

_____

_____

_____

_____

_____

_____

_____

Reflection

~What does it mean? What do I do?~

Does that sound like you or your church? Do you love Jesus today more than ever? Do you love Him with all of your heart, soul, mind, and strength (Mark 12:30)? What is the motivation behind your Christian life? The only proper motive for serving Christ is a sincere love for Him. Laboring for Jesus without loving Jesus is a sin.

_____

_____

_____

_____

_____

_____

Discuss

Take a few minutes and talk to the Lord. Ask Him to help you live out your 'truth' today. Make it an honest and personal discussion. For example, *"Lord Jesus, show me if there is anything that has taken your rightful position in my life. I repent of that today. I desire for YOU to be my 'first love.' Place in me genuine passion for you, one that will burn in my heart."* Finally, ask the Lord for an opportunity to discuss with someone what you have learned today.

A FINAL WORD

Can you imagine if millions of Christians came to understand and live out the ideas expressed in this book? Faith in Christ would be tangibly and verbally expressed. Our schools, workplaces, and neighborhoods would suddenly be captured with hope. Light would invade the darkness as Christians find an eternal and weighty purpose for their lives.

This spiritual renewal and awakening could and should be; it is certainly what I am praying for, and why I wrote this book. But you don't determine what happens to the world – you determine what happens in your own life. You and you alone decide if these ideas have any impact on your life, or if you will simply go back to business as usual. But I hope you will do two things:

1. Grow in the gospel and biblical foundations through WORD journaling. I hope you will meditate daily on the Word of God and seek continually to apply it to every fabric of your life. You may be asking, "Can I use

other devotions?" Of course you can. This is not an either/or thing – it is a both/and. But I would strongly encourage you to go directly to the Word first and foremost. The Bible has stood the test of time. We simply have to get back to the Bible. Make it a priority. Because we always have time for the things that are important to us and we enjoy, what does it say to us if we claim we simply cannot find a few minutes a day to spend alone with God?

2. Actively pursue the practice of exercising Faith, Hope, and Love. I hope you understand that the Lord is working in your life. And as you abide in Him through His Word, He will develop the "fruit" of Faith, Hope, and Love. God wants to move us all to this place where our life just teems with fruit, where we live passionate, pure, and purposeful lives.

I believe this book will serve as a helpful tool to your growth as a Christ-follower. We have only so much time left to become what God planned for us to become. To increase activity in the wrong direction makes it all futile. We need to focus on God's Key Three.

My final word to you: Do everything you possibly can to integrate the lessons of this book into the very fabric of your life. It is not theory—it is tried and true. Remember, God's very best plan for you is that, over time, you will become a person of deeper faith, a person with greater love, and person possessing a larger hope.

ABOUT THE AUTHOR

ALAN FLOYD is the lead pastor of Cottage Hill Baptist Church in Mobile, Alabama. He has served over twenty-five years as a pastor and revitalization consultant for churches and non-profit organizations. Alan and his wife have two sons.

Wyatt House Publishing

You have a story.
We want to publish it.

Everyone has as a story to tell. It might be about something you know how to do, or what has happened in your life, or it may be a thrilling, or romantic, or intriguing, or heartwarming, or suspenseful story, starring a cast of characters that have been swimming around in your imagination.

And at Wyatt House Publishing, we can get your story onto the pages of a book just like the one you are holding in your hand. With professional interior design and a custom, professionally designed cover built just for you from the start, you can finally see your dream of being an author become reality. Then, you will see your book listed with retailers all over the world as people are able to buy your book from wherever they are and have it delivered to their home or their e-reader.

So what are you waiting for? This is your time.

visit us at

www.wyattpublishing.com

for details on how to get started becoming a
published author right away.